CARLTON E. BECK, Ph.D.

Assistant Professor of Education
Wisconsin State College
River Falls, Wisconsin

❖ Philosophical Foundations of Guidance

© 1963 by Prentice-Hall, Inc.
Englewood Cliffs, N. J.

Library of Congress Catalog No. 63-17330

Printed in the United States of America

PRENTICE-HALL, INC.   *Englewood Cliffs, N. J.*

To my wife Lorraine
and to Marcia, Larry, and Carol

. . . Every scientific method rests upon philosophical presuppositions. These presuppositions determine not only how much reality the observer with this particular method can see—they are indeed the spectacles through which he perceives—but also whether or not what is observed is pertinent to real problems and therefore whether the scientific work will endure. It is a gross, albeit common, error to assume naively that one can observe facts best if he avoids all preoccupation with philosophical assumptions. All he does, then, is mirror uncritically the particular parochial doctrines of his own limited culture. The result in our day is that science gets identified with isolating factors and observing them from an allegedly detached base—a particular method which arose out of the split between subject and object made in the seventeenth century in Western culture and then developed into its special compartmentalized form in the late nineteenth and twentieth centuries.

—Rollo May, *Existence* ✗

There is a great quotation that I can include in my dissertation. Also I should get this book, R. May seems to be quoted much in Humanism and Existentialism.

~~The quote is mistakenly referenced.~~ It ~~comes from~~ repeats in "The Discovery of Being" page 45-46, chapter 3.

Foreword

This is an unusual book in that it is the first to trace historically what the author considers to be the philosophical foundations of the guidance movement. Whereas some readers might not agree with the author concerning his philosophical and historical placement of the various aspects of the guidance and counseling movement and the individuals involved, they will probably agree that this book does present a somewhat novel perspective of guidance and counseling.

The guidance "movement" in education has been generally considered—correctly so, I would think—as an American product, and as such, it has had very much of a pragmatic tinge—pragmatic, at least, in the actual practice of guidance. On the other hand, I have the impression that over half a century ago Frank Parsons was operating much more on a philosophical concept of the nature of man than were thousands of the "let's fit the right fellow to the right job" vocational counselors who followed him. In a similar fashion, when guidance became involved and enmeshed with the mental hygiene and mental health movement, many were concerned with what we might think of now as the existential man. However, the empiricism of the behavioral scientist proved so strong that many of the "personal" counselors in schools differed from their fellow "job" counselors only in the sense that they were working with problems instead of jobs. In both cases, man was unfortunately left sitting off in a corner, quite alone. In this book, Beck brings the emphasis to bear, not on jobs or problems or behaviors or physical difficulties, but on man—the "one-piece man."

Some readers may be somewhat skeptical about Beck's five stages of development—the amorphous stage, the prescriptive stage, the nondirective stage, the phenomenological stage, and the existential counseling stage—and many of his presuppositions will be questioned. Nevertheless, for far too long school counselors have worked with bits and pieces of man, and Beck performs a notable service in this book by presenting a strong position for the thought that man is more than a bundle of flesh and bone and muscle, and more than a set of problems or behaviors. He is a total complex being, he is living and emerging *now*, and he is a fellow human of worth and value and dignity.

Dugald S. Arbuckle
Boston University

Preface

This book is intended for all who are deeply concerned about human beings in times of stress and indecision. It was written to bring to light the basic presuppositions of those who have served the guidance function throughout man's history, and emphasizes recent theory and practice. Unless these basic assumptions are examined, agreements and disagreements in terminology are, at best, only superficial and can mislead sincere students. We must know what we are accepting if acceptance is to be vital.

The design of the study is discussed in the introduction. Basically, this book is an analysis of the history of ideas in guidance. Attention has been given to the social and cultural changes that have brought about these shifts in ideas.

An exciting new current of thought originating in European therapy may have a powerful impact on guidance in this country. Indeed, it may revolutionize guidance theory and practice. That current of thought has been rather fully discussed herein and has been related to contemporary thinking in guidance.

I am deeply grateful to Dr. Robert H. Beck, who read the entire dissertation upon which this book was based and who offered many helpful suggestions. Sincere appreciation, too, is due to Dr. Dugald Arbuckle, who reviewed the draft for Prentice-Hall. Neither, of course, is responsible for any errors or omissions in the final product. Many staff members at Minnesota have contributed suggestions and ideas, also, and to them I am sincerely grateful.

I am especially indebted to my wife and children, whose patience and encouragement during several long years have made this book possible.

Contents

*Proximate aims. Presuppositions from guidance literature.
Rationale for this presentation of "representative philosophies."*

*Introduction. Basic questions to be discussed. The semantic
confusion of "meeting needs." Existential psychology: Extension of phenomenology. The Daseinanalyse point of view
and related views. The mature person. Religious existentialism. Implications of existentialist thought for the future
of guidance and counseling. Suggested synthesis for the future. Theological vs. non-theological counselors. Nature of
reality. Man's place in the universe. Nature of knowledge.
Man and freedom. Worth, good, evil. Mandatory goals.*

Selected Bibliography.

Philosophical Foundations
of Guidance

❖ Introduction

No field of endeavor which touches human lives can afford to leave its philosophical presuppositions unexamined. In the *Apology* Socrates stated, "The life unexamined is not worth living." The Western intellectual tradition has affirmed the need for reflection.

This study analyzes the literature of guidance written since 1950, with emphasis on the more recent writings. The changing emphases occurring in guidance theory and presuppositions have been noted. An attempt has been then made to synthesize these stated and implied presuppositions into a representative philosophy of guidance.

Materials Used

All philosophically oriented articles and books on guidance from 1955 to 1962 have been taken into account, plus selected pertinent writings published prior to that period. The extensive literature of psychotherapy has been cited only when it was pertinent to guidance, as normally defined in the literature.

Composition

This study consists of five major sections:

1. Changing presuppositions of the guidance function throughout history
2. Review of the current literature in the philosophy of guidance
3. Presuppositions of modern guidance

The first of these sections describes how the *functions* of guidance were performed and viewed before the advent of the formalized field called "guidance," and the presuppositions under which those performing the guidance functions operated.

In Chapter Two is a brief review of the articles and books which pertain to guidance philosophy in modern times, noting "movements," changing emphases of research in the field, and presuppositions which have been stated or implied in the literature.

Chapter Three is devoted to a discussion of the presuppositions drawn from the literature. An attempt is made to synthesize these into a "presuppositions framework" representative of guidance today.

Chapter Four proposes a new synthesis of the presuppositions which, it is hoped, will provide a more consistent and operable framework for guidance theory. In many respects Chapter Four is the *raison d'être* of this study.

Chapter Five, summary and conclusions, is self-explanatory.

Need for the Study

In recent guidance literature several major writers have expressed concern about the paucity of explicit statements dealing with the philosophical foundations of guidance. They felt that basic assumptions and guidelines have been ignored for many substantial reasons, but that such omission was detrimental to the future of guidance as a profession.[1]

A recent survey of guidance literature confirmed the concern of these writers. *The Review of Education Research*, April 1957, showed that books and articles dealing, even tangentially, with the philosophy of guidance were very scarce.

Moynihan summarizes the situation:

> It was the opinion of the committee for this issue of the *Review* that there was a need for a chapter on the philosophy of guidance. However, an investigation of the literature during the past three years proved somewhat disappointing, nor was there any significant improvement when the search was extended to embrace a five-year period. Not only is there a notable scarcity of explicit references

under the title, "Philosophy of Guidance," but where reference is made, the treatment is schematic and limited to a paragraph or two in many current textbooks, or to what amounts to *obiter dicta* in the periodical literature. To be sure, principles are stated and assumptions made, but formal discussion of what the philosophy of guidance is or means is surprisingly lacking. Kneller has stated that if textbooks are any criterion, we have little proof that guidance counselors are fully aware of the philosophical assumptions toward which they gravitate or that they are seriously interested in them.[2]

It was to this lack of systematic philosophical treatment that this study was addressed.

Perhaps the most thorough attempts at treating the philosophy of guidance have come from Cribbin,[3] Wrenn,[4] Lloyd-Jones,[5] Mathewson,[6] and Rogers.[7] Other writers have attempted thoughtful examination of one or two aspects of guidance philosophy.

The paucity of literature in this important phase of guidance needs explanation. There were several key factors.

Immediacy vs. Theory Formulation

Wrenn isolated what may be the chief factor in the lack of guidance literature dealing with philosophical assumptions, stating that guidance has grown so quickly and has had so much thrust upon it in its formative years, that there has been no time for careful, unified theory or for scholarly, detailed statements of philosophical foundations. Wrenn made an analogy between the sudden growth of a new suburb with its "streets-to-be-paved-now" problems and the "something-must-be-done-now" problems of guidance.

If home building is extensive and expansion rapid, the need for streets will be a demanding one. Concrete or asphalt roadways may be laid so rapidly that careful grading and the preparation of foundations is neglected. The streets may carry the traffic and keep people out of the mud, but they will soon break through in spots, or fail to adapt to the runoff in time of heavy rainfall. Such streets may further lack consistency of material and structure—with one block of concrete and another of blacktop, gutters here but no gutters there, street signs on the curb in one block, and on posts in another.

An observer viewing this system of streets might cry aloud "expediency," "opportunism," and even "graft," but of course such an observer is not likely to have been present when the pressure was on. . . .[8]

4

Other Factors

In this same article Wrenn stated that in addition to the problems of immediacy, literature on the philosophy of guidance has not kept pace with other facets of guidance because of scarcity of research specifically oriented to a guidance services model; the lack of interest in matters of a technically philosophical nature by "symptom-oriented" practitioners; and the lack of training in general philosophy found in counselor-preparation programs.

Wrenn has touched on what well may be basic factors accounting for the dearth of literature concerning the philosophical bases of guidance. The *early* practitioners simply had no time for speculative writing or for philosophical analysis; they were men and women dedicated to a job to be done, a job of enormous proportions. *Present* practitioners have had no preparation in general philosophy in their counselor-education programs. So many other disciplines of "more *direct*, more *immediate* usefulness" have had to be studied. Philosophical formulations have been relegated to the fringe areas of guidance literature. There they have remained, although there is a strong desire on the part of acknowledged leaders in the field to encourage philosophical analysis of guidance.

But, to quote Pasteur, "Without theory, practice is but routine born of habit. Theory alone can bring forth and develop the spirit of invention." This does not mean that guidance has operated without any theoretical bases. All counselors and professors who have prepared counselors have had some sorts of theories by which they have operated, but the literature has not revealed these in depth. There have been many statements of technique, but few of basic philosophical assumptions.

Because so many have counseled so long from so many different (and usually unstated) philosophical points of view, the logical approach seemed to be the identification of common presuppositions. It appeared that only in this way could guidance present a coherent theoretical-philosophical foundation.

Earlier Attempts at Theoretical Analysis

James Cribbin examined approximately two hundred guidance textbooks commonly used in the preparation of counselors. His survey dealt with the literature from 1935 to 1950.[9]

Cribbin's study summarized the tenets of guidance shared by virtually all authors in the field. That his summary has been representative of the field was rather well established, if the amount of criticism of his presentation found in the literature was any indication of its acceptance. No one has seriously challenged his findings, which will be presented in Chapter Three of this study. His work was the only full-scale attempt at survey and assumption-finding to date.

The writings of Cribbin, Wrenn, Lloyd-Jones, Williamson, Allport, Mathewson, Rogers, and other thoughtful writers in the field have concentrated chiefly upon four phases of the philosophy of guidance: (1) the presentation of common tenets of various leading authorities in counseling and related fields, (2) the stripping away of semantic confusions, (3) attempts to align the philosophy of guidance with one of the systematic schools of philosophy (chiefly instrumentalism), and (4) their demands for more research to validate generally held assumptions. Their contributions in these areas pioneered the quest for a philosophy of guidance which will provide system for the future. The major works of these authors dealing with the philosophical aspects of guidance are listed in the Bibliography.

Limitation of the Bibliography

The review of the literature in this study includes only those books and articles which deal with the philosophy of guidance or with other pertinent theory-oriented phases of guidance. Inclusion of most of the *technique*-oriented writings would have served no real purpose. If, by extrapolation, a technique-oriented article or book served the purpose of this study, it was included. If a given article was discussed at length elsewhere in this study, reference to this fact was made and only a brief, pertinent summary of it appears in the review of literature.

Approaches Suggested by the Literature

Two leading writers[10] in guidance literature have suggested that perhaps the basic step in formulating a philosophy of guidance would be to align guidance beliefs with one of the known systems of general philosophy such as realism, idealism, pragmatism, or some other.

The two writers mentioned above have attempted such an alignment with interesting results. Lloyd-Jones[11] had tentatively aligned guidance with Deweyan instrumentalism. Wrenn[12] had stated that the counselor often seems torn between several contending philosophical schools of thought; Wrenn presumably casts his ballot for instrumentalism. Both approached this alignment from the viewpoint of key concepts which *as they were stated* (e.g., "Change is the basic fabric of the universe," "The worth of the individual is of paramount importance . . . ," etc.) were common both to the leading writers of guidance literature and to the philosophical school to which they compared it.

It is the contention of this study that perhaps a more effective alignment might have been obtained by presenting first the philosophical *presuppositions* of guidance and of the several systems which seemed to "fit best," and to attempt then to arrive at a consonant system. Without examination of the more basic question, "What does a given statement of belief presuppose?" the apparent agreement in terminology and catch-phrases tends to be only a verbal agreement, perhaps a glossing over of seriously incompatible, bedrock differences.

At any rate, the search for a known philosophical system which "fits" the common tenets of guidance authorities was a serious pursuit. It was not merely a search for a label. If such a "fit" could be found, the guidance theorists and practitioners could glean the fruits of long, thoughtful contemplation and writings of the school of philosophers it represents. Guidance then could build on the accumulated philosophical heritage of which it is a part, and could begin to examine itself critically, and, more important, systematically; it would have a nexus in which to focus.

Such a search for system among known philosophical schools of thought could serve another extremely important purpose as well. *If* there were one set of basic presuppositions and one system toward which modern guidance is oriented, and *if* that position *necessarily excluded* some of the premises which were personally vital to a given person contemplating guidance as a life's work, then, perhaps, the systematic presentation of the position early in counselor education might save time, effort, and frustration for a person who *could not accept* the basic framework within which he must work. Also, such presentation might encourage and reinforce a novice seeking to find out whether his deepest feelings are consonant with those of the recognized leaders who speak for the field of guidance. If *no single set* of presuppositions were required, this, too, should be known by the novice to straighten his thinking from the outset.

The vital questions of this study, then, are:

1. What have been the presuppositions of guidance throughout man's history?
2. What changes, if any, have taken place in these basic presuppositions, and why?
3. What presuppositions are necessary to guidance today?
4. Do these presuppositions fit any known system of philosophy?
5. What do these presuppositions imply for the future of guidance and counseling?

Footnotes

[1] *Viz.*, Wrenn, Mathewson, Moynihan, Lloyd-Jones.

[2] James F. Moynihan, "The Philosophical Aspects of Guidance," *Review of Educational Research*, N.E.A., April, 1957, p. 186.

[3] James F. Cribbin, *An Analysis of the Theological, Philosophical, Psychological, and Sociological Principles of Guidance Presented in Textbooks Since 1935* (New York: Fordham University Press, 1951).

[4] C. Gilbert Wrenn, "Philosophical and Psychological Bases of Personnel Services in Education," *N.S.S.E. Yearbook*, LVIII, Part II, 1959.

[5] Esther Lloyd-Jones, *Student Personnel Work as Deeper Teaching* (New York: Harper & Row, Publishers, 1954).

[6] Robert H. Mathewson, *Guidance Policy and Practice* (New York: Harper & Row, Publishers, 1955).

[7] Carl Rogers, *Client Centered Therapy* (and others) (Boston: Houghton Mifflin Company, 1951).

[8] C. Gilbert Wrenn, *op. cit.*, pp. 47-48.

[9] James Cribbin, *op. cit., passim.*

[10] *Viz.*, C. Gilbert Wrenn, and Esther Lloyd-Jones.

[11] Lloyd-Jones, *op. cit., passim.*

[12] Wrenn, *op. cit., passim.*

CHAPTER ONE

❖ Changing Presuppositions in the Guidance Function Throughout Man's History: An Overview

Formal guidance, as a separate professional field of endeavor, was a development of the early twentieth century.[1] However, the ideas underlying the aiding of an individual in his time of need are perhaps as old as mankind. "Mental disorder, in one form or another, has been recognized from time immemorial." [2] The *functions* which guidance today serves (personal choices, vocational problems, interpersonal relationships, and aspiration level, to name only a few) have been performed in various ways by various agents since earliest times. Man has always been concerned about his plight in a seemingly adverse world.

> Primitive man, with his ignorance of the phenomena about him, was both mystified and frightened . . . yet he found a very simple explanation for it . . . in the various natural occurrences he saw . . . gradually these . . . became deified. . . .[3]

As civilization replaced savagery, he became concerned also about the plight of his fellow men in their struggle, their problems of existence.

Mutual aid seemed a logical result of their predicaments.

Many means of alleviating life's uncertainties have been tried, with varying degrees of success: superstitious practices, edicts of tribal authorities, religious beliefs, reason, opinions of the group, science, and others. A rather complete account of this in regard to the "aiding" of neurotics, psychotics, and others has been written by Henderson and Gillespie.[4]

Cultural anthropology has given us insights into man's continuing search for guidance in his way of living. Every known tribe, past and present, has attempted to further its ways of life, aid its young to become full members of society, and to eliminate some of the pressures of living. Comparative studies of religion, puberty rites, and education have confirmed this.

> In order to continue a society must transmit its beliefs, values, skills, and other behavior expectations to its new members.[5]

Presuppositions in Tribal Life

Custom and tribal law, a product of custom, dictated the limited area in which primitive man made his choices.

In prehistoric societies the accent was upon survival; the mores and the religious rites were addressed primarily to that end. All else was of necessity secondary. To the primitives, man was viewed as an object of little power in an overpowering environment.

> The frightened man was driven into the realm of fantastic imagery. He knew very little, and the little he knew was merely an awareness of self. . . . He populated the world with imaginary beings . . . useful ones, injurious ones.[6]

The world about him was almost totally beyond his control; the world was irrevocably "there," cold and unyielding. It was a hostile place, a lonely place. The task of man, therefore, was to come to terms with that which he could not change. One had to adapt or perish.

Insofar as man acted in ways which aided his own survival probabilities and those of his group, he was deemed "sensible," a "good" member of the group. In that he acted in ways not conducive to survival of his group, to that extent he was deemed "evil" or "undesirable" by his society.

One only need consult the language of primitive peoples of both yesterday and today to see how man's "power" was viewed by primitive societies. Man did not control his ultimate destiny; powers greater than he decreed other vital aspects of his existence to a large and unalterable degree, as well as his demise.

We can find among the most primitive peoples . . . a belief in a supernatural, impersonal force, moving all . . . causing all important events. . . .[7]

Decision-making, then, hinged upon survival and adaptation; this was the state of man's thinking about life choices until the Greek Age. All advice given and all actions taken were addressed to the basic ends of *living* and *living with less stress*.

The presuppositions about man and his world were simple and in the main undoubted during this period of man's history.

GUIDANCE, IN THE BROADEST SENSE OF THE TERM, WAS THE AID GIVEN BY ONE PERSON TO ANOTHER, OR BY A GROUP TO ITS MEMBERS, IN SEEKING WHAT WAS THE "BEST" COURSE OF ACTION IN TERMS OF SURVIVAL OF THE INDIVIDUAL AND THE GROUP. It took the form of advice, group decree, or religious exhortation. The term "guidance," of course, did not enter the primitive scene; the *functions* of guidance were present in the above stated forms. The goals of each individual were similar to those of today: live, and live with less stress; the goals of the group were group survival and stability.

Primitive religion indicated how powerless man felt in the face of the universe. Man felt called upon to communicate with omnipotent beings (even the term "beings" is anthropomorphic) who presumably could change his destiny for the better. Supplication, sacrifice, and elaborate ritual seemed the logical means by which man could entreat the gods to aid him. There were few, indeed, who doubted the supernatural, for it offered security.

The Greek Outlook

Man's constant struggle against the hostile phenomena of his universe continued. The polytheism of ancient Greece was another attempt to explain natural phenomena, and Greek worship rites were a continuation of man's belief that supernatural beings control man's destiny and can be entreated to intercede for man. But by the advent of the Greek Age, there were those who discerned the anthropomorphic conception of the gods and questioned the advisability of entrusting man's fate to ritual and supplication. Xenophanes, for example, wrote:

If oxen or lions had hands and could paint and produce works of art as men do, lions would paint the forms of gods like lions, and oxen like oxen. Each would represent them with bodies according to the form of each.

Later he states:

So Ethiopians make their gods black and snub-nosed; the Thracians give theirs red hair and blue eyes.[8]

These observations, made in the sixth century B.C., began a great and continuing controversy over the role of man in his world. If gods merely were created by man in the image of man, then there was ample room to doubt the teachings of the oracles and "holy" men of the day and of past days.

No less real and pressing was the problem of how to live.

If advice given even from religious sources was open to question, what advice, what ways of living were "right," desirable? The literature of Greece in the pre-Christian era is filled with man's speculations on the great problems of living. Versions of what constituted the "good life" varied widely, from the individualistic, self-centered outlook of the Sophists to the pursuit of essences expounded by Socrates and Plato. The ordinary Greek turned to his elders for advice on living.

Plato's Views on Man and Society[9]

Plato, of course, wrote nothing addressed directly to guidance. But from his views of the world, the good society, the nature of man, and the nature of values, it is possible to extrapolate reasonable implications for "guidance" in his time.

Plato, of aristocratic birth, felt that men should find their rightful places in society via a system of education. The influence of men, their social roles, their occupations, and their styles of life should be determined by intellect. Plato proposed a system of education which, if carefully followed, could select those best fit to lead the society—the "philosopher kings"—and could result also in lesser men's finding their optimum levels of operation (for the good of their society and for their own personal happiness). In today's jargon, Plato can be said to have proposed a "ladder" system of education—a "one track" system of successively more difficult and abstract levels of learning. Social status and occupation within the society were to be determined by how far one was able to progress up the educational "ladder."

Plato outlined a "lower school" curriculum which would entail folktales, gymnastics, music, games, and other studies.

After this stage of schooling came further education for those who were deemed worthy of progressing to the next level. The judgment as to who should be permitted to enter the successive stages of education was to be that of the teacher. "Vocational and education counseling" became a very simple matter under the Platonic educational system. The teacher was the social agent who was charged with performing the guidance functions.

Under Plato's system, those who were not adjudged "academically able" became tradesmen, foot soldiers, merchants, and the like. Those who went on from Plato's basic curriculum to his "cadet school" studied all those subjects which were necessary for military leadership. The studies became increasingly difficult as the "cadet school" progressed. Those who found the more advanced level of study quite difficult were, as in the basic school, "counseled out" of the curriculum (i.e., not allowed to continue past the "cadet school" level). These men became military officers of greater or lesser rank and were charged with the defense of their country.

For the very able students who survived the rigors of all previous levels of education, Plato recommended an extremely high-level, abstract curriculum: advanced mathematics, the more complex forms of the arts, science, philosophy, law. The goal of this last school was the selection of those who would lead the society: the philosopher kings. These were to be the most able minds of Athens, the policy makers, the direction givers.

Since the ultimate goal of education was finding the optimum role of everyone for the ultimate good of the whole society, Plato felt that education ought to be state controlled and state financed.

Of importance is the distinctive feature of what might be termed Plato's "advancement or drop-out" policy. The teacher, who presumably was more adept at making judgments about education than the student, made the decision for society as to which child should continue to what level. It was the sacred duty of the teacher to see that only the best minds, the minds capable of taking up the quest for the Good Life, Beauty, Truth, and Justice, should be allowed to study in the higher levels of education.

Plato's presuppositions were clear. Leading entailed giving direction. Those who were best fit to lead should lead, via their demonstrated ability to cope successfully with ideas, but not all men were capable of leading.

Plato presupposed a Grand Plan, an "archetype" of man's mundane affairs and phenomena. Understanding this pre-existent Grand Plan was man's highest task. The world of ideas was "there"; through contemplation and reason the ablest minds of men might find a way of living which would best befit man.

Under Plato's system "vocational guidance" became synonymous with the teacher's considered decision based on academic performance in a pre-established curriculum. The finding of each man's proper occupational level was of paramount importance to Plato. The welfare of society rested upon it.

The assumptions Plato made were clear. Men's abilities differed widely. The task of society, through the educational system, was to select leaders, and to choose men of x abilities to hold x jobs in the society. If the system (curriculum) were ideal, there would be no place for a vocational or educational counselor as men today conceive those roles, since the system would have performed the function of vocational selection. Perhaps there might have been room for a counselor in roles ancillary to the major purpose of the school, but "conservation of talent," to use the modern phrase, would have been accomplished by the academic program itself.

Plato's conception of a "closed system" universe, one which contains *pre-existent* truths to be discovered through logic, observation, and contemplation, persisted in various forms throughout the centuries. It is a position still held in the modern world in an only slightly modified form by some respected intellectuals (cf., Theodore M. Greene's idealism in *The Fifty-Fourth Yearbook of the N.S.S.E.*).

Significant Changes in Presuppositions

There were significant differences between the presuppositions of the early tribal peoples and those of Plato. The early tribal peoples presupposed a group of gods who somehow set the conditions of the universe and apparently could be prevailed upon to change conditions at their whim. Man was viewed as a being of little power. His only hope was to seek the help of the gods through ritualistic means. Plato presupposed a fixed world of ideas which existed and moved in accordance with certain immutable laws, laws which were accessible to man's reason, and therefore subject to his skillful use from what he knew of them. Man was not regarded by Plato as an omnipotent creature, but was viewed as having great potential to alter his lot in the face of adversity. "Man thinking" could lead a life which "fit" his potential, which would fulfill his role in the pre-existent Grand Plan of the Universe.

Men who could not fathom the ways of intellect were to follow the advice and edicts of those who presumably could do so. To Plato it was obvious that some men have within them the potential to deal with the mysteries of the universe and man's relationships to it; others have only the potentials for certain socially needed jobs demanding skill. The direction of society should be in the hands of the former. Plato's ultimate end was the Good Life and the Good Society, as herein described.

An Alternate View of Social Aims

There were many Athenians who balked at an "absolute-seeking" world view such as Plato represented.

The Sophists and their successors had preached that man ought to take care of his own interests, accumulate whatever wealth and power he could, and seek his pleasures in this life. Theirs was a more popular doctrine. It was consonant with the times. It was more immediate, it was easier to understand than "essences," a "Grand Plan," and the other abstractions of which Plato spoke. It was an appealing type of world view. Education was viewed as an individual matter, chosen and financed by the individual for individual's own profit.[10]

Long after the deaths of both Plato and his pupil, Aristotle, the ideas of "Man the Thinker" were in contention with the conceptions of "Man the Seeker after Wealth and Power." The former views presupposed man as thinking, active participant in a pre-existent Grand Plan; the latter, a creature of passions not too far removed from animals who could look forward to no existence save the one in which he was now involved, and to no fulfillment of a

"Grand Plan"; life had no meaning except what man put into it via his own personal satisfaction of appetites.

These two contending streams of thought persisted in modified forms throughout the pre-Christian era, and rose again in the only slightly altered guise of Christian Idealism vs. Paganism when the Christian era began.

The early Christians postulated a "closed system" universe governed by the laws of one God; the non-Christians held various positions, but basically the majority followed the world view held by the Sophists.

The acceptance of either view created problems for individual men and for their leaders. The persistent problem of the welfare of the individual man and the welfare of the state had to be met.

Conservation of Talent: Charlemagne's Plan

In the ninth century Emperor Charlemagne was faced with an ever-present problem of rulers: the optimum use of talent.

The social setting in which conservation of manpower takes place determines the means to be employed. Charlemagne's approach to the problems in his society closely paralleled the approach of other totalitarian leaders.

His was a class-oriented view, but one which, unlike Plato's, conceived of leadership in a different way, stressing a "given" authority. This theory came to be known as the "Divine Right of Kings." The major similarity between this ninth-century system and the pre-Christian system of Plato was that both sought to find a position for each man consonant with his "natural abilities." Both sought thereby to strengthen their respective societies, but with different ends in view. Plato sought an aristocracy of the intellect; Charlemagne sought capable minds to assist the "given" ("rightful") aristocracy whose rule was "preordained by God." Guidance today is faced with many problems which echo these sentiments in modified form.

Charlemagne's society was one which had two distinct classes— virtually castes—of the privileged and the subservients. His goal was not to do any sort of "equalizing"; he merely desired to find talented young men who were working below their capacities as peasant farm laborers and to use their talents to greater advantage than as tillers of the soil.

Charlemagne sent for Alcuin, a monk in York, England, who was acknowledged to be one of the most able teachers in the Empire. He explained to Alcuin his plan for bringing together the many semiliterate public officials so that Alcuin could teach them to read, write, and study more effectively; these public officials were then to go back to their positions and instruct their subordinates in reading and writing. The subordinates would then instruct peasant youths who showed "keen mind and ready spirit" in the literary skills. This was not intended as "universal education." It was an attempt by Charlemagne to upgrade his officials and thereby to make possible the better employment of bright peasant youths in the service of the Empire.[11]

Almost three hundred years before this plan was set into operation, Emperor Justinian had closed all schools except the Christian schools. Charlemagne realized that his hopes for literate officials called for a much more effective (and much more widespread) system of education than prevailed in his day. He spent much time giving encouragement to the setting up of schools in connection with parish churches in various parts of the Empire. The selection of students to receive literacy training was left in the hands of parish priests. This selection presumably was to be done on the basis of the subjective opinions (perhaps based on observations in work situations) of the priests in charge of the schools.

The *function* of academic and vocational guidance, then, was to be served by the parish priest. He selected those of "higher caliber" who had the potential for acquiring literacy skills and for using them to serve the Empire.

To Charlemagne there were classes of men meant to follow and others meant to lead. Birth was not just a cosmic accident; God had ordained the privileged to rule and the less fortunate and less talented to work to carry out the orders of the privileged. It was the task of the privileged to rule and that of the less fortunate and less talented to work to carry out the orders of the privileged. It was the task of the privileged classes to offer leadership and thereby protection to the masses. The world was viewed as a cosmic system governed by immutable laws. Man's task was to survive in the hostile world and to prepare for the next (spiritual) world revealed through religious teachings.

Effects of the British Poor Laws of 1601

In the centuries that passed between the reign of Charlemagne and the sixteenth century, mankind was faced with horrible diseases, numerous wars, and violent class consciousness. The literature of the times depicts the attitudes of the people. At no time in human history, perhaps, have men been more thoroughly convinced that life on this earth was unfriendly, cruel, and impersonal; that man was powerless in the face of nature; that men were destined at birth to be what they would be. This is seen most vividly in the British Poor Laws of 1601.

Pauper Apprentices

In 1601 the British government passed legislation providing for children from "bad homes" (children of alcoholics, paupers, idlers, prostitutes, and other undesirables) to be taken from their homes as early as feasible and apprenticed to tradesmen who would teach them a useful trade plus literacy skills.[12] England, worried about the rise in crime rates, the increase of drug traffic, prostitution, beggars, and delinquents, felt that the most effective and least expensive way to safeguard against antisocial behavior was the teaching of a trade or other salable skill to children who then would become, theoretically, self-supporting. This "education" of the "public charges" became equated in the popular mind with "pauper's education." Later, when "free public education" was proposed in the American colonies, it was debated by those who remembered the Poor Laws and the effects of their brutal implementation.

Many of the tradesmen chosen to be masters over the children were cruel, semiliterate men who took the children only for selfish reasons; having several apprentices lightened one's work load. The lot of these unfortunate children is portrayed in English literature. Many of them committed murder or suicide to escape their master's heel. Many ran away. Few grew up in healthy environments.[13] The word "education" as applied to this sort of training was a mockery.

Few children learned to read and write. "Real education" was education in the liberal arts; it was for those who could afford it by virtue of wealth and position. "Pauper's education" galled many of those young men who grew up as "twenty-four hour a day apprentices." They never forgot it, even when some of them later came to America. As was stated in the previous paragraphs, the struggle for a common school supported at "public expense" was an uphill battle against old memories and old grievances.

There was no attempt at vocational guidance of any sort in the Poor Laws. The process was purely judicial. No interests, attitudes, aptitudes, or abilities were taken into account. While some children did adapt to the training, the over-all program left much to be desired. It was cold, impersonal.

The human personality was looked upon as anything but sacred. A man's nature was determined by birth. Men were very different. Some, of genteel birth, were destined to have; others—commoners —were to have not. This same attitude can be seen in religious tracts of that period. Man's lot was predetermined on this earth; only through planning well for an afterlife could man ameliorate his lot.

Education was highly selective and expensive; it was for the wealthy and the well-born. Few people really felt that the masses needed education or could profit by it. One learned a *trade* via apprenticeship *training*, not by *education*. Training was sufficient for commoners.

The Nature of Man, 1601

The basic question asked by Socrates in ancient Greece again arose: What is the nature of man? If mankind were merely a self-aggrandizing, opportunistic animal, perhaps the measures taken in the Poor Laws to treat him as such were fitting.

One of the most thorough treatments of the subject in that day is found in the writings of John Locke. Basically, Locke proposed a neutral type of nature for mankind in his famous *tabula rasa* concept. The implications of his ideas for guidance will be discussed at length in Chapter Three. Locke hinted at several key concepts which later formed the foundation of the vocational guidance movement.

It is at this point in history that two divergent streams of philosophical thinking emerged which profoundly influenced the present philosophical controversies in psychology and in guidance. Gordon Allport describes this as the "Locke-Leibniz Split" in philosophy.[14] This important controversy, also, will be discussed in Chapter Three.

Functions of Guidance in the New World

As has been previously stated, formal guidance is a product of the late nineteenth and early twentieth centuries. However, it is necessary to understand the thinking of the culture out of which guidance evolved. The *functions* performed by counselors today were performed, albeit crudely, even in colonial times.

Spiritual and moral guidance was provided by the family and the church in the early colonies. No formal attempts at psychological understanding were made; edicts based upon religious doctrine provided the guidelines for action. Insofar as man conformed to the image of the "good life" presented by his church and mirrored by his family and community, he was considered "good." Nowhere is this more clearly seen than in the colonial schools.

Colonial Schools and Guidance

In this country the doctrinal outlook of Christianity in its several forms provided the nucleus of education and the standards for personal conduct. One need look only so far as the materials used in the early New England schools to find substantiation for this statement.

The Massachusetts Hornbook, the famous *New England Primer*, early texts by Thomas Dilworth, Ezekiel Cheever, and others, attest to the philosophical tone of the early American schools.[15] No attempt was made to separate religion from education; religion *was* education. One learned to read in order to study his Bible.

The nature of man was viewed as being stained by "original sin." "Free will" was preached and taught to the people by such distinguished Puritan ministers as John Cotton, Increase Mather, Cotton Mather, and Jonathan Edwards. "Free will" in a simple form was a necessary presupposition in Puritan thinking, since the crux of Puritan living was the *responsibility* of the individual for his own actions. "Ought" implied "can" to the Puritans, and presupposed, therefore, free will and choice in matters of daily living.

The task of the schools in the training of youth was quite clear. The basic statement of their role:

1. Provide literacy skills for the laity in order that they might reinforce their belief in the doctrines of the church by reading the Sacred Writings.
2. Teach the doctrines of man's destiny as set forth by the Puritan Church to provide guidance in the lives of the young people.
3. Maintain and encourage, by force if necessary, adherence to Puritan beliefs.
4. "Cull out" (this unfortunate phrasing is found even in the later writings of Thomas Jefferson) the best scholars in order that the "best minds" might be encouraged to enter the ministry.

The presuppositions here are obvious: There are certain truths pre-existent which man must learn about and act upon. These truths already had been discovered through revelation and reason. "Eternal" values, since they were regarded as absolute, were to be learned and acted upon, not questioned. Nowhere is this more clearly seen than in the sermons of the "Puritan Divines" such as Michael Wigglesworth and Jonathan Edwards.

Wigglesworth described the bleak Puritan outlook. Written in poetry form, his book depicted the basic teachings of the Puritan church and its strict insistence upon obedience to its teachings. Perhaps the most typical and revealing example of this is the poem involving the babes who had died before having been baptized. The babes pleaded before the great, angry God of the Puritans to be spared, since they had not really had time to obey the Commandments, and that the fault was not totally their own. The answer given by the wrathful God is a classic statement of the views of Puritanism:

Ye sinners are, and such a share as sinners might expect
Such shall ye have, for I do save none but mine own elect.
Yet to compare your sins with those who lived a longer time,
I do confess your sins much less—but every sin's a crime.
A sin's a crime, therefore in bliss you may not hope to dwell,
But unto you I shall allow: the easiest room in Hell.[16]

Edwards delineated the Puritan outlook on mankind in his sermon, "Sinners in the Hands of an Angry God," a work found even today in one of the most widely used high-school textbooks in American literature. He portrayed men as small specks upon the hand of a wrathful God. This God, upon whim, opened his hand, shook it, turned it over above the Bottomless Pit of Hell. The moral of Edwards' sermon was that each man had to "cling tight to God" (i.e., to the teachings as presented by the Puritan church); there was no guarantee of salvation, but the only way one had a *chance* for being saved was by strict "holding" to God.

The foregoing selections spell out only too clearly man's plight and task. Man was a creature conceived in sin through no fault of his own, yet he was to spend his whole life becoming worthy again in the sight of a strict, demanding God. Man was under the control of forces outside himself, except for a small measure of freedom of choice given to him in making the daily decisions of living. But *upon those choices* in how he would live his life depended his destiny in an afterlife.

The Puritans asserted that in the ultimate analysis man was alone before his God. The words of his religion and the mutual aid of his friends and neighbors were all he had of comfort. Man existed to work hard, to "keep the faith," and to save his soul in the manner prescribed by authority. The task of the school and of all his elders was to see that he understood his tasks, and that he responded to them as expected.

The problem of "free will" and the problems of man's destiny have been sources of theoretical difficulties in the literature of all fields which deal with human behavior. Anxiety and guilt feelings, common phenomena in guidance and therapy work, are often traceable to conflicts involving these questions. The thinking of leaders in guidance on these points as exhibited in the literature will be discussed in Chapters Two-Four. These questions are of prime importance in the formulation of a philosophy of guidance.

Role of the School

The influence of the teachings of religion continued to dominate the schools for the first three hundred years of American history. There were important voices raised in dissent: Jefferson, Franklin, Horace Mann, W. T. Harris, William James, John Dewey. It was not until the twentieth century, however, that the most significant attempts were made to change the practices in this regard.

The school in society is still the bulwark of middle-class values, still held responsible to the community for passing on the cultural heritage, still held responsible for "character training," even though doctrinal teaching is discouraged both legally and ethically. Herein have lain many of the personal and group conflicts so familiar to the thoughtful writers and practitioners in the field of guidance.

Influence of the American Frontier

To many settlers on the American frontier, *formal* education was precisely that: education in *forms*. The "book l'arnin'" which was assimilated by the upper classes of the East was held to be useless in the physically demanding, environment-battling, simple society of the westward-moving pioneers. Latin and Greek literature had little meaning for the frontiersmen.

The values of the frontier had their roots in the soil tilled by the frontiersman. Man worked hard, treated his neighbors with respect so long as they responded in kind. The mutual aid pioneers gave each other is legend. Religion was a personal theory to these sturdy people. It was not the infrequent appearance of a circuit-riding preacher, nor the Sunday meeting in the more settled areas. It was a personal relationship to God. The values which fit the life of the frontier were accepted; the more formal "values" of church life were either rejected or disregarded as not applicable.

A man or boy "just tried his hand" at various occupations until he found his niche. One tried, and either succeeded or failed—in school or in life. There were always well-meaning advice givers and clergymen with whom to talk, but no one trained for the function was to be found. Man made his own decisions. Trial-and-error attempts in the area of vocations resulted in many wrecked, unhappy, misspent, unproductive lives and much loss in time and money. But there was always a new start for those with courage; there were new places to go, places to begin again.

Formal Guidance Appears

As education became more available in America, it became apparent that certain problems were arising which the teacher by training, inclination, or lack of time could not or would not handle. A brief reflection upon the rapid developments in our history will call to mind dozens of "complicating" factors which led to the development of guidance and student personnel services. These developments were well illustrated by several authors in the field of guidance. The accounts most useful to a study of this type are, perhaps, of the sort written by Barry and Wolf [17] and by Hitchcock, *et al.*[18] Among the chief developments which led to the establishment of formal guidance in America were these:

1. Co-education
2. Shift from rural to city living
3. Advances in transportation, and therefore in geographic mobility
4. Accessibility of education
5. Changing concepts of education
6. Industrialization and diversification
7. Immigration
8. Civil War
9. Freeing of slaves
10. World War I, World War II, Korean conflict
11. International tensions
12. Changing international policies
13. Depression and recessions
14. Sectional differences in attitudes toward education
15. Psychological research, especially in testing
16. Theoretical formulations by psychologists
17. Mental health movements
18. Key writings on mental illness and anxiety
19. Support for basic research from foundations and individuals
20. Concern for conservation of talent
21. Need for technical personnel in industry
22. National defense considerations
23. Federal legislation, especially the G.I. bills
24. Miscellaneous influences

This list of influences was drawn primarily from the above-mentioned books. The list is a composite. While many categories listed do overlap, and although other developments might be noted which contributed substantially to the establishment of formal guidance in this country, the list points up interpersonal, intergroup, and intercultural tensions which demanded resolution or amelioration. The formulation of guidance, student personnel work, counseling, and whatever other terms have been used to denote the services which attempt this resolution and amelioration, was a sudden process, a searching one, a confused one.

The Vocational Guidance Phase

Many guidance writers recognized the publication of a modest book by a Bostonian social worker, Frank Parsons,[19] as the beginning of the vocational guidance movement in this country. The book, intended to aid those who would attempt to counsel students in planning their futures, provided a rationale for vocational guidance in its formative years.

The Parsons Method

Parsons proposed a three-step method of counseling clients with regard to vocational choice: (1) Know the student; (2) Know the world of work; and (3) Match the man with the job. This approach, as explained by Parsons and his followers, appeared logical. The counselor had to know the likes, dislikes, abilities, experiences, and lacks of the counselee; he had to have wide acquaintance with the world of occupations, the prerequisites for getting and holding jobs of many sorts; he had to be possessed of keen "matching" ability, once the first two steps of the rationale had been completed.

The implications for the philosophy of guidance and the presuppositions of such an approach were far-reaching and are discussed in Chapter Three. It is perhaps sufficient for the purposes of this chapter to state that the suggestions of Parsons made necessary the development of tests and other instruments to facilitate "knowing the traits" of the student. It was not enough for one attempting to counsel to follow "general impressions" or "logic" alone. Observations, according to Parsons, had to be made objectively. For the field of guidance—and for psychology—a new period was launched. It was a new era with new presuppositions. It was the era of trait psychology.

As will be demonstrated in Chapter Three, the dominant features of trait psychology were a "correspondence theory of truth," a reliance on actuarial prediction, and the eventual realization that man reacts as a whole organism. But the latter realization came much later.

Tests and Testing

Parsons found that the psychological instruments and techniques needed to study individuals were virtually nonexistent. Aside from the speculative, subjective writings in psychology there were no real indices of what we now term aptitudes, interests, or self-concepts. Even intelligence testing was in its infancy. There were only two intelligence-testing instruments being standardized to any extent.

Without any means of measuring "traits"—and the existence of these traits was presupposed—the "objective" three-step process of Parsons bogged down. The field was ripe for psychological research. The development of tests to measure these pre-existent traits became a significant trend in psychology in America and elsewhere. This was perhaps the most significant development for guidance up to the 1930's. Guidance was attempting to move from the informal, theologically influenced, intuitive type of "folk medicine" in choice making to an objective, test-centered, formal analysis of problems dealing with interpersonal (and, often, intrapersonal) difficulties.

Donald Paterson[20] reported that three other events which occurred at approximately the same time as the publication of Parsons' book did much to further the guidance movement. The first of these was the serious study of retardation in education, thus centering attention of researchers on the area of individual differences in any given random-sampled group.

Paterson stated that the second major development was an inquiry into the problems of industrial turnover rate and the causal factors behind quitting, sporadic employment, and misemployment. The need for something to be done in remedying these social problems was well established.

The third factor in Paterson's account was G. Stanley Hall's invitation to Sigmund Freud to speak at Clark University, thus introducing Freudian ideas to a number of leading figures in American psychology. Freud was known but not widely accepted in this country until after this address. Paterson felt that this lecture was influential in furthering the serious study of psychology in this country.

Paterson also stated that Parsons and his immediate successors furthered the "know the world of work" phase of inquiry by producing many books, monographs, and pamphlets dealing with the requirements of various occupations. Parsons and his colleagues in social work did not attempt to contribute to the "know the man" phase of the problem, since they felt that this type of pursuit might best be undertaken by psychologists.

Paterson termed counselors who *today* follow the Parsons model as "arrested in their professional development." He felt that such procedures were regrettable in view of all the objective instruments and accumulated data on behavior which have become available.

Many new currents in psychological research had important bearings on the infant guidance movement. The years immediately preceding and following World War I were especially fruitful.

Yerkes and Scott developed the first large-scale personnel classification system for the United States Army. The system was based upon classification cards upon which were entered many data. Their work was done essentially on the Parsons model: pertinent information about the individuals was matched with the descriptions of jobs to be filled in the army.

One basic psychological instrument involved in the collection of data was the intelligence test. The forms used were the Army Alpha and the Army Beta tests, designed for use with literate and illiterate servicemen, respectively.

In the 1920's the intelligence test and the newer aptitude tests became more widely accepted in education and in industry.

Books about the choice of an occupation[21] later became common. Several able writers produced easy-to-read pamphlets and monographs about occupations.

The development and use of standardized achievement tests in the secondary schools and in higher education followed.

The writing of books and monographs and the designing of achievement tests both have been pursued quite seriously, chiefly through the efforts of leading institutions of higher learning, organizations such as the American Council on Education, and private corporations.

Paterson[22] reported that the armed forces, private industry, municipalities, and universities have followed the Parsonian model in dealing with employee selection and placement. He stated that such a manner of selecting and placing workers is at best inadvisable. His major objection appears to be the mechanistic matching of men and jobs.

> Mere knowledge of industry and of vocational information, books and pamphlets is not enough. The modern guidance worker must be thoroughly grounded in psychology, in research and statistics, and in clinical procedures. An M.S. degree in psychometrics or its equivalent would appear to be a minimum essential. The Ph.D. or its equivalent would appear to be a desirable qualification. It goes without saying, of course, that this newer type must also possess the personality traits that characterize those who are successful in dealing with people in face-to-face situations.

This description was quite remote from the training recommended for counselors by Parsons, also reported by Paterson.[23]
Parsons described his counselor-training program thus:

> At least three hours a week of laboratory experience . . . (in vocational guidance) . . . formulating the counsel believed to be appropriate for the solution of the specific problem presented by each case. . . .
> To enter the vocational course a man must have excellent character and ability, good manners and address, at least a high school education or its equivalent, and a satisfactory experience of two years or more. . . . He must have attained the age of twenty-five years, unless very mature at an earlier age. The time required will be one, two, or three terms. . . .

Much more might have been stated in this chapter concerning the history of guidance and related areas of study: the role it played in and after the Great Depression, the role of guidance in national defense, in rehabilitation of World War II veterans, the program of government funds available for the training of counselors under the National Defense Education Act, and other important yet less widely known aspects of guidance. To have done so, however, would have been beyond the purpose of this study. The bibliography indicates sources for further reading in the history of guidance and student personnel work.

Status of Guidance Today

The *Review of Educational Research*[24] stated that guidance today has become widespread, well-recognized, and a hope for survival, but that it is at a loss for guidelines and theories. Chapter Two was drawn from the philosophical literature in guidance. The succeeding chapters present the presuppositions drawn from the literature, and synthesize these into a proposed framework for the future.

Footnotes

[1] Frank Miller, *Guidance Principles and Services* (Columbus, Ohio: Charles E. Merrill Books, Inc., 1961), p. 3.

[2] D. Henderson and R. Gillespie, *A Textbook of Psychiatry* (London: Oxford University Press, 1948), p. 1.

[3] O. S. English and Stuart Finch, *Introduction to Psychiatry* (New York: W. W. Norton Company, 1954), p. 3.

[4] Henderson and Gillespie, *op. cit.*, pp. 1-14.

[5] Wilbur Brookover, *A Sociology of Education* (New York: American Book Company, 1955), p. 4.

[6] Gregory Zilboorg, *A History of Medical Psychology* (New York: W. W. Norton Company, 1941), p. 27.

[7] Bronislaw Malinowski, *Magic, Science and Religion* (Boston: The Beacon Press, 1948), p. 3.

[8] Reported in S. E. Frost, Jr., *Basic Teachings of the Great Philosophers* (New York: Barnes & Noble, Inc., 1942), p. 112.

[9] This entire section is based on Plato's views on the "good society" as set forth in *Republic*.

[10] Kenneth Freeman, *Schools of Hellas* (London: Macmillan & Co., Ltd., 1922), Chap. 5, *passim*.

[11] Frost, *op. cit.*, p. 241.

[12] William Drake, *The American School in Transition* (Englewood Cliffs, N.J.: Prentice-Hall, Inc., 1955), p. 74.

[13] William Drake, *The American School in Transition* (Englewood Cliffs, N.J.: Prentice-Hall, Inc., 1955), p. 74.

[14] Gordon Allport, *Becoming* (New Haven: Yale University Press, 1955), p. 14.

[15] A well-documented source for the history of colonial education is Drake, *op. cit.*, Chap. II.

[16] Michael Wigglesworth, *Day of Doom*. Reported in Drake, *op. cit.*, p. 16.

[17] Ruth Barry and Beverly Wolf, *Modern Issues in Guidance-Personnel Work* (New York: Columbia University Press, 1957).

[18] A. A. Hitchcock, *et al.*, "Milestones in the Development of Personnel Services in Education," *N.S.S.E. Yearbook*, LVIII, Part II, Chap. XI, 1959.

[19] Frank Parsons, *Choosing a Vocation*, 1909, as reported in *Introduction to Student Personnel* by Edmund G. Williamson and J. G. Darley (New York: McGraw-Hill Book Company, Inc., 1937).

[20] Donald Paterson, "The Genesis of Modern Guidance," reported in Farwell and Peterson's *Guidance Readings for Counselors* (Chicago: Rand-McNally Company, 1960), pp. 103-105; originally in *Educational Record*, Vol. 19 (1938), 36-46.

[21] (e.g., Crawford and Clement's *The Choice of an Occupation* and Parker's *Books About Jobs*, a bibliography.)

[22] Paterson, *op. cit.*, p. 107. Paterson's work is herein closely paraphrased.

[23] Paterson, *loc. cit.*

[24] Moynihan, *loc. cit.*

CHAPTER TWO

❖ Review of the Current Literature in the Philosophy of Guidance

Paucity of Materials

The number of articles and books dealing with the philosophical aspects of guidance was extremely disappointing to the leading authorities in the field.

Many of the articles and sections of books which are reviewed here are only tangentially philosophical, but have been included to present as true a picture as possible of what presuppositions have undergirded practices and stated beliefs of leading theorists.

To date, there has been only one doctoral dissertation (excluding my own) which dealt in detail with the philosophical aspects of guidance, and it surveyed the literature prior to 1950.

No attempt has been made to include the countless articles dealing with *method* in counseling. Allusion to these has been made wherever pertinent in Chapter Three.

The Review of Educational Research for 1957 and the same publication for 1960 presented a *total* of only eighty articles and chapters of books which spoke at all of the philosophical aspects of the field. The *Review* stated that many of these items would not qualify as strictly philosophical.

Since the 1960 *Review* was published, only a few additional articles have been written which are of a philosophical nature.

Articles from 1952 to 1957

From the period of 1952 to 1957 only forty philosophical articles were found in the literature of guidance or in that of closely related fields. Perhaps the most thoughtful and complete work of this type done during this period was that of Carl Rogers,[1] Gordon Allport,[2] James Cribbin,[3] Robert Mathewson,[4] and Esther Lloyd-Jones.[5] Of these, Cribbin's contribution was the only doctoral dissertation.

Cribbin's dissertation contains detailed analysis of two hundred textbooks in guidance from 1935 to 1950 in which he drew together the statements common to virtually all of the texts concerning purpose, ethics, and common principles of guidance. The dissertation was exceptionally well documented. The fact that it was written for a religiously oriented institution may have influenced the viewpoint of the writer, but no one has seriously questioned his compilation of "common denominators in guidance through 1950."

Rogers, the chief spokesman for nondirective or client-centered counseling, clarified and revised in a minor degree some of his concepts from his previous books, *Counseling and Psychotherapy* and *Client-Centered Therapy*. His major contention remains that the client can make his own choices, given an accepting atmosphere and freedom from threat.

Allport again made his pleas for personalism in counseling and therapy, and strengthened his case by scholarly analysis of divergent trends in psychological thought dating from Locke and Leibniz. He discussed phenomenological concepts and the newer philosophy of existence as it was pertinent to the problems of human anxiety. His analysis of the "emergent personality" was perhaps the most thorough treatment of the self-concept in the forty articles and books from 1952 to 1957.

Mathewson's book contained one very significant attempt to explain contemporary guidance philosophy in terms of field theory. His psychological account of modern guidance theory was clear and challenging, but the chapter on philosophy of guidance became primarily credo and a description of guidance as a learning process involving the total organism.

Lloyd-Jones and Smith discussed the need for the identification of guidance assumptions with one of the extant schools of philosophical thought. They presented the opinion that Deweyan instrumentalism is the philosophy which fits best the common beliefs and experimental work in guidance. Their thesis was that if some existing school of thought in philosophy could be shown to fit the guidance model, then that philosophy could be studied by guidance practitioners and theorists as they think through aims, procedures, and research designs. If such an identification were accomplished, the benefits of having a systematically stated position in philosophy would be obvious.

There appeared to be certain real inconsistencies in trying to identify instrumentalism with guidance. This is discussed at length in Chapter Three. However, the *approach* of identification of a philosophy which is consonant with guidance was a real contribution.

Articles by Shoben[6] and Murphy[7] were primarily exhortations for guidance writers to become more aware of the philosophical bases of their profession. Shoben[8] elsewhere attempted to find common focus on problems from various theoretical positions concerning human behavior.

The *Yearbook of Education* for 1955[9] raised important points with regard to counseling and guidance in other countries. It discussed certain basic assumptions made by all who counsel, whatever the social setting.

Mathewson[10] wrote of universally valid moral values, social responsibilities, and spiritual considerations in guidance. He cited no evidence for their being "universals" in the philosophical sense, other than "accumulated race experience." This in itself was worthy of discussion. It involved a commitment to a particular type of knowledge claim.

A trend toward increased concern with guidance in the realms of ethical and religious values was identified by Moynihan.[11] The presuppositions, both stated and unstated, of such activities needed examination. Moynihan identified several writings as being indicative of this trend. He mentioned Arbuckle,[12] Benezet,[13] Curran[14] and Hardee.[15] To his list might also have been added Cribbin's works, discussed earlier in this chapter, and several other works by those committed to counseling from a particular religious group's point of view. Some of these are discussed in Chapter Three as examples of the religious-spiritual values orientation in guidance and the implications that such positions might have in determining a philosophy of guidance. The presuppositions inherent in such positions needed to be analyzed. It was interesting to note the great similarities in both goals and procedures, as well as in presuppositions, between these neo-spiritual counselors and the Puritan fathers of the seventeenth century, discussed in Chapter One of this study. Hardee postulated a commitment of counselors in the giving of moral counsel.

Dressel [16] attempted, as did Lloyd-Jones and Smith, to identify the field of guidance with a systematic philosophy already known to the fields of general and educational philosophy. He too arrived at instrumentalism, equated with Deweyan pragmatism, as the philosophical model best fitting the aims and procedures of guidance. Again, this positioning was done by the juxtaposition of key words and phrases common to both, not by examination of presuppositions.

Parody [17] recommended "integration between classroom teaching and guidance," as did many others, but he spelled out what this meant in unique terms, and recommended deliberate action to achieve this integration, rather than assuming that it would take place as a matter of course. This approach had interesting implications for the formulation of a philosophy of guidance.

Miller [18] followed an approach rather common during the days when guidance was striving to gain recognition as "scientific" by attempting a model-construct involving energy exchange. The common practice of patterning a social science after natural sciences in order to win respectability as a true science has been followed in nearly all of the newer social sciences. However, Miller's approach contained some key presuppositions which had to be analyzed.

In an exchange between Rogers (previously noted in this chapter) and Walker, [19] the latter stated that Rogers' theories and practices are the natural successors to those of Rousseau. His case, convincingly stated, again revealed interesting presuppositions. Walker appeared concerned about the plausibility of reconciling Rogerian philosophy with that of the so-called "clinical counseling" writers. This concern has been discussed. Such reconciliation would serve an important need in the philosophy of guidance, even though research had demonstrated that there is more difference among the members of either "school" than between the two schools themselves; nevertheless, the presuppositions were at issue here, not the way in which a given individual put them into practice.

Moynihan[20] stated that:

> Throughout the literature there are recurrent overtones of a fundamental concept of man as a psychological organism, conative, responsible, self-directive, and a flexible participant in his own development and in the societal processes of our American democracy, which concept has been in the literature for some time. . . . Guidance workers continue to couple this concept with a respect for what man is and can become as well as with methodological approaches which seek the complete actualization of man's nature, physical, social, intellectual, emotional, and spiritual, both as an individual and as a member of society.

Moynihan's documentation of this statement was limited to four sources during the five year survey which he was discussing. Two each supported the respective halves of his statement (the break is indicated by ellipses). However, careful perusal of technique-oriented literature and of the general textbooks in guidance (especially those of Mathewson, McDaniel, and Rogers) provided supportive evidence that Moynihan had stated the case correctly.

Cribbin's[21] study of the period 1935 to 1950 agrees in all respects with the paragraph cited by Moynihan except in regard to "spiritual nature." The emphasis on spiritual values in counseling appeared to be a product of the 1950's. If the number of pages of print devoted to man's "higher nature," "spiritual being," and the like, was any indication of counselor concern, the trend was toward this type of endeavor. However, the semantic problem with the term "spiritual" needed clarification. Presuppositions involving such a concept had to be carefully spelled out. If the term were used in a sense understood by traditional religious groups, or if it were used in the sense of most of the existentialist writers, the presuppositions and ontological outlook would vary.

The citations which Moynihan offered in support of his statements about the "overtones" in guidance literature have been listed (*infra*, footnotes 22 and 23). It was interesting to note that both citations originate from sources concerned primarily with higher education, and that those compiling the viewpoints are usually associated with the "clinical counseling" positions rather than the nondirective point of view. Why Moynihan included either reference in his survey of a "period of five years" (presumably 1951-1957) was not mentioned in the article.

Moynihan's statements about "actualization of man's nature" have been documented by the sources in footnotes 24 and 25. There had been no rejection of the contentions made by these sources in the literature of guidance up to 1962. Therefore, it could be rather safely stated that this is the guidance "position" on the matter. To state this did not obviate the semantic problem, however. This is discussed at length in Chapters Three and Four. The presuppositions underlying such a position had been hinted at in the literature, but needed spelling out.

Both Morse[26] and Super[27] gave careful consideration to the effect of the social setting in which guidance takes place. Super pointed out that whether a developmental emphasis or a rather firm "problem solving" emphasis in guidance comes about is largely a function of the socioeconomic conditions and the political framework within which guidance workers must operate. Morse, in another article written with Lee,[28] stressed the importance of reconciling group living and its problems with allowing the potentialities of each individual to be developed.

Bordin[29] introduced the interesting premise that the personnel services worker is an agent of social policy, an administrator. If each man is to realize his own potential, individual "life style" of coping with himself and society (and if, as Bordin stated, this is desirable), the justification for psychological workers in addition to personnel services workers, who speak necessarily for society, is clear. The questions raised by the acceptance or nonacceptance of Bordin's justification are fraught with philosophical implications.

The two remaining works mentioned by Moynihan, Pepinsky and Pepinsky,[30] and Kneller[31] raised questions of values and goals.

Most of the other articles which were listed in Moynihan's survey dealing with philosophy of guidance literature were tangential. Those seven articles included by Moynihan, but not described herein, were of interest, but it was felt that they did not aid in the determination of the philosophical presuppositions of guidance, and they are therefore excluded from this study.

Philosophy of Guidance: Literature from 1957 to 1960

The years 1957-1960 brought no increase in the *number* of books and articles which dealt with the philosophy of guidance, and no dissertations on the subject. However, there were a few indications that this field will be investigated. Some of the chief writers in the field gave thoughtful attention to the theoretical bases of guidance, and two new texts were written in an attempt to pull together the implications of guidance theory and practice into a coherent, consistent framework. One chapter of the N.S.S.E. *Yearbook on Personnel Services in Education* was devoted to the philosophical and psychological bases of guidance-personnel work.

Trends

The trends in the philosophically oriented literature of guidance from its inception as a formal field of endeavor can be identified by ten categories. They are mentioned here so that current trends can be viewed in the light of previous ones.

1. Gaining acceptance as a professional field of endeavor
2. Delimiting its scope (usually expanding it)
3. Developing "Schools of Thought"

Phases 1-3 occurred from approximately 1900 to 1950. From the period 1950 to 1957, the chief phases (continuing the list above) were:

4. Attempting to reconcile the "schools" and seeking out common elements in them
5. Attempting to formulate ethical codes, and a preoccupation with questions of the relationship of man with his fellows
6. Considering the nature of man, and what this implies for guidance

The period 1950-1957 saw the leading writers in guidance turning to the literature of general philosophy and to the philosophy of education in order to work out a systematic theory. This was a significant change from the previous ten years in which theory builders turned not to philosophy, but to psychological research. The first step in this new direction was both psychological and philosophical, as might have been expected. Phenomenology, a child of both fields, provided a widely accepted model for guidance theory in this transition period.

The classic work of Snygg and Combs, *Individual Behavior,* published in 1949, was being read with interest, as was Lewin's field-theory explanations of human behavior. Neither of these became a significant part of the journals in guidance until after 1957, but the *ideas* were being discussed in seminars at Minnesota and elsewhere. Part of the initial acceptance of the "individualization" in counseling that is demanded by phenomenology might be credited as a reaction against the then current test-centeredness and actuarial-type prediction in guidance. Whatever the reasons, the work of Snygg and Combs had a significant effect on the philosophical articles and books in guidance from that time on.

The period from 1958 to 1960 saw great commitments being made, and a rapid expansion of counselor training programs. The National Defense Education Act of 1958 and subsequent legislation provided funds for the upgrading and expanding of counseling staffs in secondary and elementary schools. The chief goals of these moves were the conservation of talent and the early identification of interests and abilities as a means to strengthening our national defense.

With new demands being made on the field of counseling and guidance, the leading writers in the guidance-personnel literature called for an examination of the philosophical bases upon which counseling and other guidance activities were operating, and also upon what thoughtful bases they perhaps *ought* to operate. In the opinion of many the key writing on this subject was that of C. Gilbert Wrenn[32] of Minnesota. Wrenn spelled out his own views on the goals of counseling, and those of other leading theorists in guidance. He then attempted to relate these views to already systematized schools of thought in general philosophy. This approach, the identification of guidance with some single school of thought from general philosophy, had been tried before, but Wrenn was the first to discuss the various philosophical schools. Previous attempts at linking guidance with a philosophy had been merely the presentation of the given author's views as to which philosophy "fit" best with the views of guidance. Wrenn was the first to bring to the guidance literature a *description* (albeit brief) of various contending philosophies, thus making guidance practitioners aware of them, and attempting to stimulate them to evaluate which philosophy, if any, "fit" guidance. This was a significant step in the literature of the philosophy of guidance.

Wrenn found that instrumentalism or Deweyan pragmatism seemed to coincide with the ideas of most of the writers in the field of guidance, as had others who had attempted the same feat before him. But Wrenn raised real questions as to whether or not that philosophy was adequate for the tasks *ahead*. At that point he struck upon a key point *not* mentioned by others who had tried to "identify" the philosophy of guidance: Even *if* the instrumentalism of John Dewey described practices and beliefs in the field, perhaps the *appealing features* of that philosophy might be found in *another* system which had the prerequisites for the *future* of guidance theory and practice. At one point Wrenn hinted that another philosophy would appeal to him "if the barriers were down." With that statement he set the stage for what might result in the most important advance in the philosophy of guidance since its inception. It is toward the removal of these seeming "barriers" that Chapter Four of this study is addressed. To discuss the topic further at this point would be premature.

The continuation of the listing of philosophical trends in the guidance literature could be stated as:

7. Rather wide acceptance of phenomenology and/or field theory as the physical model for guidance
8. A comparison of the credos of leading writers in guidance with existing "schools" in general philosophy and in the philosophy of education
9. Examination of chief problems or dilemmas in guidance in the light of the "schools" or "positions" mentioned in item 8 above
10. Realization that philosophical aspects of guidance must be put in order if guidance is to meet the new challenges in which it is becoming embroiled

There was an eleventh trend which had not yet entered the journals or books in guidance. It was not included because the above list is of trends *taken from the literature* of guidance. Though several articles have implied agreement with this eleventh trend, the literature had not systematized it or explicitly stated approval of it. That trend was to be found in the work of Binswanger and others in Germany, France, and other parts of Europe, plus in the lucid writings of Rollo May in this country. Clinical and psychiatric practice have made use of a new framework; it has been slowly becoming known outside these fields. That development was termed by May[33] the *Daseinanalyse* philosophy of clinical treatment. This will be discussed at length in Chapter Four. This development may provide the unifying force needed for what Wrenn indicated were the new challenges of guidance. DASEINANALYSE PHILOSOPHY IS PERHAPS THE META-PRAGMATIC FRAMEWORK NEEDED TO "KEEP THE BEST OF THE PAST AND PROVIDE NEW DIRECTION FOR THE FUTURE."

In the research summary by Wilkins and Perlmutter[34] there were listed forty articles and books dealing to some degree with the philosophical aspects of guidance from 1958 to 1960. Twenty-eight of the forty authors listed had *not* written articles or books listed in the previous (1957) five-year survey of articles and books dealing with the philosophy of guidance. When the names of these twenty-eight were examined, it became apparent that the philosophical aspects of guidance were becoming increasingly significant to the acknowledged leaders in the field. Wrenn, Dugan, Mueller, Kitson, Mowrer, C. H. Patterson, and Tyler were all among the writers who had turned their attention to the philosophical bases of guidance during the period 1958-1960. This was perhaps an indication of a serious trend in the literature which cannot do other than profit the field.

These writings from 1958 to 1960 may be grouped under three major headings: those dealing with values, those dealing with finding a philosophical "position" for guidance, and those examining the relationship of guidance activities within the total social framework.

As stated previously, Wrenn's treatise on the philosophical bases of guidance represents the first extended treatment of guidance philosophy, although Lloyd-Jones[35] and Dressel[36] had arrived at some of the same conclusions in brief treatments of the subject.

The question of human values, both social and individual, and how they affect counseling has been a source of much confusion to counselors. Arbuckle[37] presented a serious article which raised questions about the personal ethical and religious values of the counselor and the effect these might have on the client. He reasoned that a counselor who was not possessed of a clearly defined set of values might have difficulty in his chosen profession. This same statement was made in the early 1900's by Frank Parsons, as Chapter One indicates. The issues that these men have raised are vital, and are commented upon later.

Also concerned with human values and deep life-meanings were Hagmaier and Gleason.[38] These men have attempted to combine a given set of values (Christian) with the newer findings in psychology. Their synthesis, while it proceeds from a set of pre-existent values unacceptable to some, provides an approach which could be adapted by many counselors who would wish to think through their own philosophies of counseling, but of course substituting their own "givens," whether these be empirically derived, intuitive, or whatever.

A symposium[39] published in the *Personnel and Guidance Journal* provided an exercise in semantics concerning the counselor's own religious values. The participants found several areas of apparent agreement, but it may be that this agreement was chiefly at the level of "glossy terms" rather than upon fundamental presuppositions.

Williamson,[40] in approaching the question of counselor values, stated that since the counselor cannot keep his own values completely out of the counseling situation (and this, in itself, is a major presupposition shared by most of the leading writers), the counselor ought to "put his cards on the table" and assume the role of a teacher. In this case the teaching task would be that of showing the client how to live consistently and reasonably within the framework of the values *chosen by* or *important to* the *client* himself.

If Williamson's contention that the counselor must assume the role of "teacher of values" (and this feeling is shared by many, notably by Mueller[41]), there may be a serious question as to the qualifications of the counselor to do this. It would seem that the lack of training in ethics and in general philosophy, which Wrenn and others have noted several times throughout the literature, might raise a real question for the future education of counselors. If the counselor is to assume the role of "teacher of values," it would seem that he must have at least some preparation in the field of philosophy upon which to draw.

Continuing in the vein of values in counseling and other guidance activities, Walters[42] recounted the oft-told tale of the attempts of guidance to gain recognition as a science by copying physical-science models of theory and research. Walters felt that the extreme empiricism, perhaps necessary in the early days of gaining acceptance, is being and ought to be modified. Human values seemed rather different in kind from behavioral analysis based on a physical-science model. This view, that the extreme empiricism of guidance might well be modified, was in contradistinction to the views of Bordin.[43]

Wrenn[44] examined the question of the counselor's dual responsibility to his client and to his society. He stressed that certain religious and spiritual values must be taken into account. Until the terms "religious" and "spiritual" are stripped of the ambiguity in meanings found in the literature of guidance, Wrenn's presentation stands in opposition to, or in ambivalent position toward, other well-regarded spokesmen in the field. Wrenn's views in this matter will be discussed later.

Hobbs[45] examined certain aspects of determinism as they apply to responsibility in human behavior. Since this problem of "oughts" vs. "cans" has recurred so often in the literature, Hobbs's thoughtful article is "must" reading for all serious counselors and therapists.

Spates,[46] while not guidance-personnel trained, wrote a book important to any counselor who recognizes the importance of human values in the selection of a vocational or professional field, continuation or discontinuation in it, and "work tone" while engaged in various positions. He raises points which have important implications for guidance theory. He seems to supplement many of the ideas of Donald Super in his work on vocational choice theory.

Guidance and Society

The relationships among several vital factors in guidance composed much of the philosophical literature. The relationships coming in for most comment were: (a) the counselor's role as an agent of society, (b) his role in the restructuring of a client's views, (c) his preparation to undertake such restructuring, (d) the needs of society and the needs of the individual, and (e) counselor ethics.

Smith[47] questioned the assumption that the accumulation of "healthy," productive individuals must necessarily produce a "healthy" society. If this view becomes widely accepted, the present presuppositions of guidance will need thoughtful revision. Smith's statement anticipated, perhaps, some of the tenets of *Daseinanalyse* theory, discussed in Chapter Four.

Rockwell and Rothney[48] raised some interesting points concerning the social views of early guidance pioneers. All of the pioneers discussed, it would appear, were to some degree social reformers, and Rockwell and Rothney spoke of "Guidance workers who know best what is good for society . . ." as an assumption held by the pioneer theorists in guidance. Also identified were evidences of a type of realism in values. The description of the beliefs of the pioneers in guidance presupposed a correspondence theory of truth, a belief found not infrequently in recent literature, but often only by inference or extrapolation from recommended practices.

The approach by Rockwell and Rothney opens up what may prove to be a highly significant field of endeavor: the consideration of the social views of the leaders in the formation of guidance theory. Perhaps many trends and suggested directions in theory and practice are more the result of these personal value commitments than of considered evidence.

Wise[49] presented the idea that "events general to higher education will more powerfully affect the student personnel field than will specific developments of thought or technique within the field." He cited census data and other statistics on married students, extension of equality of opportunity, the return to college of older students, and changing patterns in the financing of higher education. He called for a thorough study of the historical roots of guidance and a knowledge of the society in which guidance has grown. (This same demand has come from Wrenn and others, and has been in part answered by Chapter One of this book.) He would not limit this study to the usual "history of guidance" accounts of the past three or four decades as is usually done when guidance writers refer to the history of their enterprise.

Harrison[50] proclaimed the duty of the counselor to identify the gifted child as early as possible "both to himself and to his world," thus implying that this type of student has the duty to perform to his highest potential, and that the counselor has an ethical charge to fulfill the identification function.

Mathewson[51] set up a fourfold strategy for guidance. He cited real "models" upon which guidance appeared to be operating, and offered the assumptions underlying each strategy; e.g., in what he termed the "selective-distributive strategy" of guidance, the assumption was made that:

> Individuals cannot learn about themselves, accept themselves, and control their choices and behavior to any significant degree, but rather choose and act on the basis of deep-seated traits which are the product of inborn temperament plus experiential conditioning.

As another assumption, he stated that "many individuals will consciously direct their choices for . . . personal objectives . . . that may or may not relate in collective summation to social needs or requirements."

Several other assumptions of the various modes of operation in vogue in guidance today were discussed with attention to their underlying assumptions. The assumptions in this article are important, and are discussed at length in Chapter Three.

Maehr and Stake[52] reported an important example of how deductive reasoning unsupported by substantiating evidence can lead counseling awry. Their work pointed up the importance of constantly re-examining "obvious" truths in the context of rapidly changing social institutions—in this case, religion.

The American Personnel and Guidance Association[53] issued a statement of policy regarding the school counselor, his preparation and selection. The statement, compiled by leaders in the field of guidance, but also sensitive to the (solicited) comments and suggestions of all persons interested in guidance-personnel work, made an important contribution to "what guidance says," consolidating in one source the many statements found here and there in many articles and books.

Rogers[54] analyzed the possible effects of our ever-growing knowledge of conditioning and its possible uses "for good or for evil purposes." His article evaluated and came into serious conflict with the behavioristic *Walden II* (*q.v.*) of Dr. B. F. Skinner. Rogers pointed out positive advantages of freeing man to arrive at his highest potentials. He expressed real fears of possible enslavement by rigid conformity to power groups which might be using conditioning techniques.

Skinner's views were also analyzed. His message was essentially that many means of conditioning are available, and will become increasingly so, to psychologists to make possible the attainment of virtually any type of society; all that is necessary is that social goals be specified.[55]

Rezler[56] stated the "commercial intent" of college students, and attributed this to parents who had no well-ordered set of values of their own to pass on to their children. She points to the ". . . need to have values, more compelling values than living up to the Joneses and making money; they would need to believe in self-expression, independence, hard work; self-discipline, and making one's own decisions as reflected in [a group of students acquiring a broad cultural background, doing independent study]."

Brown[57] discussed the ethical problems involved in releasing data about a student to prospective employers and to other agencies of society. Brown's report presented a survey of practices involving deans and their policies regarding the release of "confidential" information. Serious problems were turned up, and posed as unanswered questions. Other writers have speculated on this delicate relationship between civil rights and the public good.

Ginsberg[58] laid bare three very basic assumptions of guidance. He presented material vital for the formulation of a philosophy of guidance. In the same article he gave examples of actions by counselors which *appeared* consonant with the objectives of guidance, but which in the long run were defeating the basic premises and goals which guidance hopes to serve.

Philosophical Position for Guidance

Williamson[59] stated that guidance-personnel work has arisen out of problems, not deductively from a system of philosophy. He felt that this has been a primary strength of the whole enterprise. He reiterated points made earlier by Lloyd-Jones and others that student personnel work and guidance have reflected a general education tone, that the tone has been set primarily by the institution in which it has operated, and that the philosophy of instrumentalism seemed to be most congruent with the beliefs of guidance and personnel workers.

The statement by Williamson that instrumentalism seemed to represent best the beliefs of guidance theorists is called to question in Chapters Three and Four of this book.

Patterson[60] joined several other key writers in guidance who felt that the phenomenological model best described counseling theory and practice. In this he shared the usual nondirective aim of striving for "individual freedom and action" by actualizing and clarifying self-concepts. Patterson[61] agreed with Williamson that the values of the counselor would enter into the counseling situation willy-nilly (see footnote 40).

Shoben[62] telescoped the generally accepted beliefs and operating principles of guidance into a short, clear statement. This was helpful, since Chapter Three of this book deals with "what guidance says" in an attempt to find a consistent philosophical system for the field.

Wrenn[63] listed several beliefs held by counselors. These warranted careful examination from the standpoint of philosophical assumptions inherent in them. The statements by Wrenn appeared to reflect very accurately the position of most of the writers in the field, and were helpful in determining a philosophical basis pertinent to guidance.

Milliken[64] advanced hypotheses and conclusions which were fraught with assumptions as to the effectiveness of counseling in the elementary school, and were common to many writers in the field. The blanket recommendations about making the students "more realistic" toward occupations appeared to ignore the recent literature of psychotherapy regarding self-concepts and threats imposed upon the self by forced or carefully guided congruence with test results. The whole area of earlier and more intensive counseling rests upon assumptions which have not, it is felt, been based upon sufficient experimental evidence. One rather basic assumption, made time and again in the construction of tests and attitude inventories, is especially in need of attention by theorists.

Preference or attitude inventories are usually standardized by giving a group of items to "successful" performers in a given field (lawyers, doctors, social workers); then, if a client shows interest or attitude patterns very similar to those of people successful in a given field, this is taken as an indication that he might consider that field as a life's work. Perhaps there is a real joker in the deck in this type of procedure, since it assumes that the interest patterns of the successful lawyer, for example, were the same WHEN HE WAS THE AGE OF THE CLIENT—usually, this would mean pre-college age—as they now are. It would seem that a much more valid, albeit more difficult, way of approaching interest patterns would be to examine the interest patterns of teen-agers who then later *become* successful lawyers. At our present stage of knowledge, we are uncertain whether it means anything if a prospective high-school-age attorney-candidate has the same interest patterns or preferences as a mature, successful attorney. The approach suggested herein seems logically more consistent, but must await experimental verification.

Selden,[65] in a thoughtful study of self-concept and level of aspiration of delinquent and nondelinquent boys, found consistent evidence that the boys in trouble had faulty self-concepts in far greater proportions than the nondelinquent boys. This bears out the findings of others in self-concept studies; Selden further found, however, that the level of aspiration exhibited by these troubled boys is much lower than the levels shown by the nondelinquents. He postulated that this was due in part to fear of failure. Selden's findings are consonant with the newer insights of *Daseinanalyse* theory to be discussed in Chapter Four, especially in regard to life-anxieties.

Glanz[66] identified the goals of guidance-personnel work with those of theorists engaged in human relations and group dynamics research. If this hypothesis were true, and if this viewpoint were shared by many others in guidance, many philosophical questions would arise. For example, a study by Dupuis[67] has revealed several philosophical assumptions of group dynamics which would be most unacceptable to the major theorists in guidance. If the two fields do proceed from the same philosophical base, then both fields must do a real self-evaluation. Glanz is correct that both fields (guidance and group dynamics) pursue several goals in common, but the philosophical framework of two groups pursuing the same goals need not be at all identical, as will be shown in Chapter Three.

Mowrer,[68] in a thoughtful article exploring accepted basic premises of psychology, psychotherapy, and counseling, postulated a new conception of the mind-body problem which had interesting implications for the philosophy of guidance. The relationship between Mowrer's ideas and the usually accepted phenomenological model of human behavior must be reconciled or re-evaluated. Mowrer, together with Rollo May, Viktor Frankl, Dugald Arbuckle, Gordon Allport, Leona Tyler, William Luijpen, C. Gilbert Wrenn, Carl Rogers, and C. H. Patterson, has been speaking out for a return to genuine concern for individual man, for sincere commitments, for the uniqueness of life-styles. The work of these writers will bear careful attention as guidance moves toward a new stage of development, as described later in this book. They are perhaps the precursors of what might be the revitalization of the field of guidance.

Tyler's article[69] hinted at an existentialist approach to counseling, but did not use the term. She spoke of the right and responsibility of each counselor to think through his own theories of therapy, philosophy, religion, and other important phases of personal value-orientation.

Smith[70] questioned the assumption that the accumulation of "healthy," productive individuals must necessarily produce a "healthy society." If this view becomes widespread, the present presuppositions of guidance will indeed need thoughtful revision. Smith's statement anticipated some of the findings of *Daseinanalyse* practice, discussed in Chapter Four.

Gruen,[71] also anticipating some *Daseinanalyse* thinking, questioned the way in which our society regards creativity and uniqueness. This article, by its statements and by its general tone, gave evidence that the newer European concepts in therapy and counseling might receive enthusiastic acceptance in this country. The presuppositions must be made explicit, however, if the acceptance is to be genuine and vital.

Samler[72] presented support for the views of Allport regarding personal emphasis in counseling and therapy as he discussed the "tone" of guidance philosophy and the basic assumptions made. Samler made several clear statements of what the literature of guidance indicates for philosophical foundations. He spoke in particular about the responsibility of the counselor, the model of human behavior generally accepted in guidance work, and attempted a new synthesis. Samler's thinking, too, led in the direction of *Daseinanalyse* assumptions; these were shared by many of the major writers, as has been previously indicated, although none have used the term to date, with the exceptions noted later in this book.

Shoben[73] underscored Allport's plea for personalism in counseling by discussing the present emphasis on "client responsibility" in the writings of guidance and therapy.

Mowrer[74] depicted several aspects of personal responsibility and related this to the idea of sin. The work of Mowrer and most of the other major writers in the field of guidance and therapy indicates a serious questioning of the behavioristic orientation found in recent years. Most of these theorists are not satisfied to view man as merely the pawn of forces beyond his control, a creature with no genuine choice-making powers. It is this dissatisfaction which has created the breach between phenomenology and existential psychology. This is discussed in Chapter Four.

Curran[75] indicated a need for the discovery of personal values by the individual, rather than the imposition of "social values." He expressed the hope that such a personal formulation would dignify the individual and further the ideals of freedom. Curran's statement expressed a viewpoint which, as did Dupuis', cast doubt on the desirability of group consensus as a criterion for action or a source of truth.

Arbuckle[76] presented a plea for the personal dignity of the individual, and criticized some of Patterson's concepts of counseling for their manipulative quality. Chapter Three shows that the views of both men can be subsumed into the more comprehensive *Daseinanalyse* thinking. Both are speaking for the dignity of man.

One of the closest approaches to the *Daseinanalyse* point of view was found in an article by Tyler.[77] She expressed dissatisfaction with certain established ideas in therapy and in counseling. Her ideas concerning the playing up of the strengths of the client, rather than trying to effect a major restructuring, is existentialist-oriented. The tone of most of her works indicates a deep commitment to most of the major principles of *Daseinanalyse* counseling, although the term has thus far not appeared in her writings.

Froehlich,[78] too, was concerned with the same problem, the tendency to equate major restructuring with counseling success. He reiterated the caution that the client must be more active in the counseling process, more self-directed, more self-determining.

Murphy and Guze[79] declared that the setting of limits in the counseling situation was *not* incongruent with the basic beliefs of many counselors. Indeed, such limit-setting could be an aid in allowing the client to come to make his own decisions. This reinforced several of Rogers' previous statements about the desirability of certain wide limits in the counseling situation. The position has important bearing on the new synthesis for guidance described in this book, and justifies, perhaps, the viewing of the counseling interview as an "encounter" (specially defined in Chapter Four), rather than as a teaching situation, a reflecting device, or an advice-giving, interpretive endeavor.

Ford[80] gave evidence supporting the contentions of Murphy and Guze, and indicated thereby that their basic presupposition warrants careful attention in any new synthesis for guidance.

Fisher and Roth[81] stated five "generally accepted views of human behavior" and attempted to reveal the structure necessary for guidance research. Their remarks had many implications for the philosophical study of guidance and its presuppositions. The five views of human behavior "generally accepted" in guidance were of special interest:

1. Factors affecting behavior can be measured independently, but function interdependently.
2. Factors affecting behavior, functioning interdependently, are generally viewed as complexes of behavior patterns, or constellations of traits, rather than single elements.
3. Behavior is over-determined. [i.e., in research employing the usual one-instrument approach the multiple-causation principle is often disregarded.]
4. Behavior is the effect of developmental sequences as well as of immediate responses. [i.e., factors which appear "related" must be assumed to exist "in depth and duration," according to the authors.]
5. Behavior is free as well as determined. Unique factors appear as the result of developmental trends as well as independent of any recognizable factors in the immediate situation. [The authors follow this statement by mentioning that "standard error" allows for unique appearance. They state firmly that "the range of possibilities is greater than the range of prediction."]

The authors of this article then presented other serious considerations which must be taken into account if guidance research is to be meaningful. The article was representative of many others occurring in the literature over the past decade, and was fraught with clearly stated philosophical assumptions.

Arbuckle[82] quoted one author who had stated that "existential anxiety is properly the domain of religion and that pathological anxiety is the proper domain of the psychotherapist." Arbuckle made a case for existential anxiety as perhaps the proper concern of the therapist, since "pathological" distress is a symptom of deeper existential longings, fears, uncertainties.

Dreyfus[83] compared Rogerian counseling to *Daseinanalysis* [sic] in Europe.

Berger[84] viewed counseling in the light of Buddhist concepts, finding some similarities in outlook.

Other articles which might be classified as philosophical were primarily exhortations, indicating a need for the examination of the basic assumptions of guidance. These are included in the bibliography.

These references were selected because they dealt either directly or by inference with philosophical issues in guidance. Primarily, they have been written by those actively engaged in guidance-personnel work activities, and have appeared in guidance or psychological journals and books. Most of the books listed have been reviewed in these same journals. Therefore, the views have been exposed to the scrutiny of virtually all leading writers in the field of guidance, and presumably represent the views which can be called collectively the guidance viewpoints on matters discussed.

Works in general philosophy have been placed in a separate bibliography. It was felt that their inclusion in the body of Chapter Two would only delay the reader in "getting on with" the philosophical presuppositions of guidance.

Neither bibliography pretends to be comprehensive; the listings are selected references which appear to aid the understanding of guidance and vocational counseling problems. The philosophical ideas drawn from these references form the basis of my synthesis.

Footnotes

[1] Carl Rogers, "Some Directions and End Points in Therapy," *Psychotherapy: Theory and Research*, Orval Mowrer, ed. (New York: The Ronald Press, 1953). See also *Psychotherapy and Personality Change*, eds. Rogers and Roslind Dymond (Chicago: University of Chicago Press, 1955).

[2] Gordon Allport, *Becoming* (New Haven: Yale University Press, 1955). (See especially material *passim* dealing with the Locke-Leibniz controversy and its implications for psychological models today.)

[3] James Cribbin, *An Analysis of the Theological, Philosophical, Psychological, and Sociological Principles of Guidance Presented in Textbooks Published Since 1935* (New York: Fordham University Press, 1951). This analysis by Cribbin covers texts up to 1950. Other works by Cribbin, which are built upon the research done for his dissertation, cover criticism of guidance and evaluation of it. These works are "Critique of the Philosophy of Modern Guidance," *Catholic Educational Review*, Vol. 53 (Feb. 1955), 73-91; and "The Modern Function of Guidance—An Ancient Christian Tradition," *Catholic Educational Review*, Vol. 52 (Nov. 1954), 510-22.

[4] Robert H. Mathewson, *Guidance Policy and Practice*, rev. ed. (New York: Harper & Row, Publishers, 1955). See especially Chap. 8, "Philosophical and Psychological Foundations."

[5] Esther Lloyd-Jones and Margaret Smith, *Student Personnel Work as Deeper Teaching* (New York: Harper & Row, Publishers, 1954).

[6] Edward Shoben, Jr., "New Frontiers in Theory," *Personnel and Guidance Journal*, Vol. 32 (Oct. 1953), 80-83.

[7] Gardner Murphy, "The Cultural Context of Guidance," *Personnel and Guidance Journal*, Vol. 34 (Sept. 1955), 4-9.

[8] Edward Shoben, Jr., *et. al.*, "Behavior Theories and a Counseling Case: A Symposium," *Journal of Counseling Psychology*, Vol. 3 (Summer 1954), 107-24.

[9] Robert Hall and Joseph Lauwerys, eds. *Yearbook of Education*, 1955, "Guidance and Counseling" (Yonkers, N.Y.: World Book Company).

[10] Robert Hendry Mathewson, "Philosophical and Psychological Foundations," *Guidance Policy and Practice*, rev. ed. (New York: Harper & Row, Publishers, 1955), Chap. 8.

[11] James Moynihan, "The Philosophical Aspects of Guidance," *Review of Educational Research*, XXVII, 2 (American Educational Research Association of N.E.A., Washington, D.C., Apr. 1957).

[12] Dugald S. Arbuckle, *Student Personnel Services in Higher Education* (New York: McGraw-Hill Book Company, Inc., 1953).

[13] Louis T. Benezet, "Guidance in Moral and Spiritual Values," *Counseling and Guidance in General Education*, ed. Melvene Hardee (Yonkers, N.Y.: World Book Company, 1955), Chap. IV, 73-99.

[14] Charles Curran, "Guidance and Counseling in Education," *Education*, Vol. 73 (Dec. 1952), 223-28.

[15] Melvene Hardee, "Moral Guidance, Our Responsibility," *Personnel and Guidance Journal*, Vol. 31 (Jan. 1953), 220-23.

[16] Paul Dressel, "The Determination of Student Needs," *Counseling and Guidance in General Education*, ed. Melvene Hardee (Yonkers, N.Y.: World Book Company, 1955), Chap. II, 26-46.

[17] Ovid Parody, "An Expanding Concept of Guidance," *Teachers College Record*, Vol. 57 (May 1956), 537-45.

[18] James G. Miller, "Toward a General Theory for the Behavioral Sciences," *American Psychologist*, Vol. 10 (Sept. 1955), 513-31.

[19] Donald E. Walker, "Carl Rogers and the Nature of Man," *Journal of Counseling Psychology*, Vol. 3 (Summer 1956), 89-92.

[20] Moynihan, *op. cit.*, 188.

[21] Cribbin, *op. cit.*, *passim.*

[22] American Council on Education, Committee on Student Personnel Work. *The Student Personnel Point of View*, rev. ed. Studies, Series 6, No. 13 (Washington, D.C.: The Council, 1949). (This is a systematic presentation of the viewpoint. The source is relatively old, but apparently not dated. The current literature reaffirms the points made.)

[23] Edmund G. Williamson, "Student Personnel Work," *Encyclopedia of Educational Research*, rev. ed., ed. Walter S. Monroe (New York: The Macmillan Company, 1950), pp. 1290-92.

[24] Mathewson, *op. cit.*, Chap. 8.

[25] Ruth Strang, "Various Conceptions of Guidance," *Yearbook of Education*, eds. Hall and Lauwerys (Yonkers, N.Y.: World Book Company, 1955), pp. 603-37.

[26] Horace T. Morse, "General Education and Individual Guidance," *Counseling and Guidance in General Education*, ed. Melvene Hardee (Yonkers, N.Y.: World Book Company, 1955), Chap. 1, pp. 3-25.

[27] Donald Super, "Guidance: Manpower Utilization or Human Development?" *Personnel and Guidance Journal*, Vol. 33 (Sept. 1954), 8-14.

[28] H. T. Morse and Dorothy Lee, "Individual Autonomy and Social Structure," *Personnel and Guidance Journal*, Vol. 35 (Sept. 1956), 16-21.

[29] Edward S. Bordin, *Psychological Counseling* (New York: Appleton-Century-Crofts, 1955).

[30] Harold B. and Pauline Pepinsky, *Counseling: Theory and Practice* (New York: The Ronald Press Company, 1954).

[31] George Kneller, "Worldly view of Guidance and Counseling," *Journal of Higher Education*, Vol. 27 (Mar. 1956), 158-65.

[32] C. Gilbert Wrenn, "Philosophical and Psychological Bases of Personnel Services in Education," *Personnel Services in Education*, Yearbook of the N.S.S.E. (Chicago: University of Chicago Press, 1959), Chap. III, Yearbook LVIII, Part II.

[33] Rollo May, *et al.*, *Existence* (New York: Basic Books, Inc., 1958). (Written in collaboration with Henry Ellenberger and Ernest Angel.)

[34] William Wilkins and Barbara Perlmutter, "The Philosophical Foundations of Guidance and Personnel Work," *Review of Educational Research* (Washington, D.C.: American Educational Research Association of the N.E.A., Apr. 1960), Chap. I.

[35] Lloyd-Jones, *loc. cit.*

[36] Dressel, *loc. cit.*

[37] Dugald Arbuckle, "Five Philosophical Issues in Counseling," *Journal of Counseling Psychology*, Vol. 5 (Fall 1958), 211-15.

[38] George Hagmaier and Robert Gleason, *Counseling the Catholic: Modern Techniques and Emotional Conflicts* (New York: Sheed & Ward, 1959). (This book, while set forth in the context of one particular religious faith, has implications for many other Christianity-oriented counselors. Basically, it is the presupposing of a set of "givens" about man and the world from which are deduced ways of handling newer psychological insights. The pattern of presentation is clear and thoughtful.)

[39] Edward Durnell, James Moynihan, and C. Gilbert Wrenn, "Symposium: The Counselor and His Religion," *Personnel and Guidance Journal*, Vol. 36 (Apr. 1958), 520-28.

[40] Edmund G. Williamson, "Value Orientation in Counseling," *Personnel and Guidance Journal*, Vol. 36 (Apr. 1958), 520-28.

[41] Kate Hevner Mueller, "Theory for Campus Discipline," *Personnel and Guidance Journal*, Vol. 36 (Jan. 1958), 302-309.

[42] Orville S. Walters, "Metaphysics, Religion, and Psychotherapy," *Journal of Counseling Psychology*, Vol. 5 (Winter 1958), 243-52.

[43] Edward S. Bordin, "A Counseling Psychologist Views Personality Development," *Journal of Counseling Psychology*, Vol. 4 (Spring 1957), 3-8.

[44] C. Gilbert Wrenn, "Status and Role of the School Counselor," *Personnel and Guidance Journal*, Vol. 36 (Nov. 1957), 175-83.

[45] N. Hobbs, "Science and Ethical Behavior," *The American Psychologist*, Vol. 14 (1959), 217-25.

[46] Thomas Spates, *Human Values Where People Work* (New York: Harper & Row, Publishers, 1955).

[47] M. B. Smith, "Mental Health Reconsidered: A Special Case of the Problem of Values in Psychology," *The American Psychologist*, Vol. 16 (1961), 299-306.

[48] P. J. Rockwell, Jr. and J. Rothney, "Some Social Ideas of Pioneers in the Guidance Movement," *Personnel and Guidance Journal* (Dec. 1960), 349-54.

[49] W. M. Wise, "Student Personnel Work—Future Trends," *Personnel and Guidance Journal*, Vol. 9 (May 1961), 704-709.

[50] Edna L. Harrison, "The Counselor's Role in the Early Identification of Gifted children," *Personnel and Guidance Journal*, Vol. 9 (May 1961), 735-37.

[51] Robert H. Mathewson, "School Guidance: A Four-Dimensional Model," *Personnel and Guidance Journal*, Vol. 8 (Apr. 1961), 645-49.

[52] Martin Maehr and Robert Stake, "The Value Patterns of Men Who

Voluntarily Quit Seminary Training," *Personnel and Guidance Journal*, Vol. 6, 537-40.

[53] American Personnel and Guidance Association, "A statement of Policy: Standards for the Preparation of School Counselors," *Personnel and Guidance Journal*, Vol. 4 (Dec. 1961), 402-407. (In subsequent issues of the Journal this article was followed by other "position" papers drawn up by the Association.)

[54] Carl Rogers, "The Place of the Person in the New World of the Behavioral Sciences," *Personnel and Guidance Journal*, Vol. 6 (Feb. 1961), 442-51.

[55] B. F. Skinner, *Walden II* (New York: The Macmillan Company, 1948).

[56] Agnes G. Rezler, "Personal Values and Achievement in College," *Personnel and Guidance Journal*, Vol. 2 (Oct. 1960), 137-43.

[57] Dirck Brown, "Interpreting the College Student to Prospective Employers, Government Agencies, and Graduate Schools," *Personnel and Guidance Journal*, Vol. 7 (Mar. 1961), 576-82.

[58] Eli Ginsberg, "Guidance—Limited or Unlimited," Address to the 1958 Convention of the American Personnel and Guidance Association in St. Louis, Missouri. Reported in *Personnel and Guidance Journal*, Vol. 9 (May 1960), 707-12.

[59] E. G. Williamson, *Student Personnel Services in Colleges and Universities* (New York: McGraw-Hill Book Company, Inc., 1961). See especially pp. 10-19.

[60] Cecil H. Patterson, "The Place of Values in Counseling and Psychotherapy," *Journal of Counseling Psychology*, Vol. 5 (Fall 1958), 216-23.

[61] Cecil H. Patterson, *Counseling and Psychotherapy: Theory and Practice* (New York: Harper & Row, Publishers, 1959. (See especially the chapter on phenomenology.)

[62] Edward Shoben, Jr., "A Rationale for Modern Student Personnel Work," *Personnel-o-gram*, Vol. 12, No. 3 (Mar. 1958), 10, American College Personnel Association.

[63] C. Gilbert Wrenn, "Some Emotional Factors in Counseling," Chapter VI, *Guidance in the Age of Automation* (Syracuse: Syracuse University Press, 1957).

[64] R. L. Milliken, "Realistic Occupational Appraisal by High School Seniors," *Personnel and Guidance Journal*, Vol. 6 (Feb. 1962), 541-44.

[65] Edward H. Selden, *A Study of Self-Structure and Level of Aspiration in Delinquent and Non-Delinquent Boys.* Unpublished Doctoral Dissertation (Minneapolis: University of Minnesota Press, 1960).

[66] Edward Glanz, "Emerging Concepts and Patterns of Guidance in American Education," *Personnel and Guidance Journal* (Nov. 1961), 259-65.

[67] Adrian Dupuis, *Philosophical Presuppositions of Group Dynamics.* Unpublished Doctoral Dissertation (Minneapolis: University of Minnesota Press, 1955).

[68] O. Hobart Mowrer, "Some Philosophical Problems in Psychological Counseling," *Journal of Counseling Psychology*, Vol. 4 (Summer 1957), 103-11.

[69] Leona E. Tyler, "Theoretical Principles Underlying the Counseling Process," *Journal of Counseling Psychology*, Vol. 5 (Spring 1958), 3-8.

[70] M. B. Smith, "Mental Health Reconsidered: A Special Case of the Problem of Values in Psychology," *The American Psychologist*, Vol. 16 (1961), 299-306.

[71] Walter Gruen, "So-called Core Culture Attitudes and the Belief in One's Own Creative Potential." Paper read at the A.P.A. Convention in Chicago, Sept. 1960.

[72] Joseph Samler, "An Examination of Client Strength and Counselor Responsibility," *Journal of Counseling Psychology*, Vol. 1 (Spring 1962), 5-11.

[73] E. J. Shoben, Jr., "Personal Responsibility, Determinism, and the Burden of Understanding," *Personnel and Guidance Journal*, Vol. 39 (1961), 342-48.

[74] O. H. Mowrer, "Some Constructive Features of the Concept of Sin," In symposium: "The Role of the Concept of Sin in Psychotherapy," *Journal of Counseling Psychology*, Vol. 7 (1960), 185-88.

[75] Charles Curran, "Some Ethical and Scientific Values in the Counseling Therapeutic Process," *Personnel and Guidance Journal*, Vol. 39 (Sept. 1960), 15-20.

[76] Dugald Arbuckle, "Counseling: Philosophy or Science," *Personnel and Guidance Journal*, Vol. 39 (Sept. 1960), 11-14.

[77] Leona Tyler, "Minimum Change Therapy," *Personnel and Guidance Journal*, Vol. 38 (1960), 475-79.

[78] Clifford P. Froehlich, "Stars, Parsons, and Clients," *Personnel and Guidance Journal*, Vol. 36 (Sept. 1957), 10-16.

[79] G. Murphy and S. Guse, "Setting Limits: The Management of the Manipulative Patient," *American Journal of Psychotherapy*, Vol. 14 (1960), 30-47.

[80] E. Ford, *et al.*, "Psychotherapy with Child Psychotics," *American Journal of Psychotherapy*, Vol. 14 (1960), 705-18.

[81] Margaret Fisher and Robert Roth, "Structure: An Essential Framework for Research," *Personnel and Guidance Journal*, Vol. 8 (Apr. 1961), 639-44.

[82] Dugald S. Arbuckle, "Counseling: Philosophy or Science," *Personnel and Guidance Journal*, Vol. 1 (Sept. 1960), 11-14.

[83] Edward Dreyfus, "Counseling and Existentialism," *Journal of Counseling Psychology* (Summer 1962), pp. 128-32.

[84] Emanuel Berger, "Zen Buddhism, General Psychology, and Counseling Psychology," *Journal of Counseling Psychology* (Summer 1962), pp. 122-27.

CHAPTER THREE

❖ Major Philosophical Presuppositions Drawn from the Literature of Guidance

Rationale

In Wrenn's pioneer attempt at formulating the philosophical bases of personnel services in education, he stressed the difficult task of "speaking for the field."

> . . . There must needs be a considered humility in such an approach, for one person's highly fallible set of convictions are spread out for public view. They are bare and unprotected, fair targets for any who wish to take pot shots at them. The reader may have a set of "importances" that he prefers. All that can be said here is that it is *this* concept of personnel work about which I am talking when we later attempt to relate philosophies and psychologies to it.[1]

Wrenn then proceeded to spell out what beliefs were held by student personnel workers as he saw them. Although space limitations precluded documentation of every point, Wrenn's portrayal of the literature, and also his evaluation of the general *tone* of the literature, appeared to be beyond question. His personal credo entered in, but was clearly labeled as such.

Wrenn's approach provided the pattern for this and the following chapter of the present study. Chapter Three is an attempt to spell out what the literature of guidance has said on various philosophical issues. This composite was formulated from the standpoint of the presuppositions underlying what appears to be its philosophical orientation.

Since the tone of the literature has changed at various stages in the development of guidance, it is necessary to state briefly the changes in major presuppositions during these stages in the history of guidance. However, of primary importance are the presuppositions inherent in guidance of recent years; partially discarded assumptions are of only historical interest to a field in search of a systematic philosophy.

The culmination of this chapter is the presentation of a systematic statement of presuppositions drawn from the literature. To paraphrase the quotation from Wrenn at the beginning of this chapter, there needs must be a considered humility in so doing, since it is difficult to speak for a field, especially when that field, by its own admission, has done so little via the literature to make explicit its assumptions.

It must be stressed that Chapter Three is not a statement of what *ought* to be, but rather of what has been the position of the writers in guidance on basic philosophical issues. Chapter Four attempts to synthesize the presuppositions discussed here, and to suggest proposals for the future.

Stages of Development

Chapter One recounted major events in the history of guidance. Those events can be summarized in a brief history of ideas in guidance theory. Guidance and related therapy work can be categorized into five periods of development: Amorphous Stage; Prescriptive Stage; Nondirective Stage; Phenomenological Stage; and the *Daseinanalyse* Stage. Tracing this line of development reveals the changes in the presuppositions under which guidance has grown.

Amorphous Stage

Since the beginning of time, men have found it necessary to work together for common protection and comfort, and have found it to their benefit to ask and to give advice when the need arose.

Such was the state of guidance, if the term can be properly applied at all to the unsystematized attempts at discharging the functions of guidance, until the late nineteenth century. No systematic theory can be assigned to this period. Much of the advice was given out of compassion for a friend in difficulty, or from a religious figure who proceeded from "givens" in his thinking, or from legal figures who spoke for society's rules and customs. Whatever the sources of advice, the basic assumption was that man could not always see his own problems clearly. In some vaguely understood way, it seemed helpful to "talk it over with others" who had a sympathetic ear and a fresh viewpoint.

Because of the nature of society, much of the guidance or advice-giving originated from religious sources: tribal medicine men, Greek oracles, rabbis, priests, ministers, or others. Society has long referred those who find difficulty in making life-choices to religious figures who presumably are "closest to" these questions. Until the advent of mechanization and urban problems, this assignment of the counseling function to religious figures filled the bill to some degree. The complexities of modern life have altered—not altared—the situation. No longer are religious figures universally deemed closest to such problems. By what criteria, for example, could it be said that a priest or minister is closest to such problems as the question of vocational choice in a complex, industrial society? Others, specially trained for the various guidance functions, had to be sought out and made available.

Up to the late nineteenth century, perhaps the closest approximation to theory was the surgical experimentation, "freeing man from trouble by letting out the demons that possessed him." The presupposition was that entities of supernatural origin existed in the body and blocked and pressed upon the normal action of the bodily organs.

We might examine the presuppositions of early religion in detail, since religious figures did much of the counseling or advice-giving, but this would only delay the crux of this study. Suffice it to say that the religious counseling presupposed a world of things which moved in accordance with laws set up by a Creating Force; that the Creating Force could change the pattern of laws; that man could, through reason, come to know what choices he "ought" to make. Revelation of various sorts played an important part in "guiding" man's reason.

Prescriptive Stage

This period had its actual beginnings with Freud. Others before him had experimented with relieving human anxiety and choice-making difficulties by hypnosis, drugs, faith healing, and punishment, but it is to Freud that we must turn for the real beginnings of the second stage of the development of guidance.

To some extent Freud's theories and practices grew out of, and built upon, the half-truths of the past. For example, there was a degree of similarity between the *surgical* freeing of demons from inside the head (the process called "trephining") and Freud's concept of "catharsis," which entailed having the subject "free" himself from pressures by "letting out" the troubles verbally. The faith relationship which developed between early Freudian analysts and their clients was little different from the reliance of the parishioner upon the ability of his priest to unravel his problems. Freud's reliance on mythological literature is another example of his using half-truths from the literature of the past to explain human behavior (e.g., the Oedipus myth).

Freud's basic ideas have been too well-disseminated to need recounting here. The presuppositions underlying his work, however, have not been so widely discussed. Chief among these were the following:

1. A deterministic world view was taken. The world was thought to exist and move in accordance with cause-and-effect "laws" of nature. A naturalistic explanation of all phenomena was held possible, given the accumulation of sufficient knowledge; the supernatural was denied existence, but was thought to be a result of pre-scientific, infantile thinking and wishing.

2. A deterministic view was taken, also, of the life of man. Man's being was thought to be composed of two definite parts, the mental and the physical. Both parts were thought to be derived from and operated by the laws of cause and effect. There were "drives," needs, and wants which of necessity determined man's actions. A restructuring of these needs was held possible, however, if man could be allowed to understand the influences acting upon him. This could be done through the prescriptions of one who was outside the organism (i.e., a therapist) and who was not subject to the forces acting

upon the client. The therapist could therefore see more objectively the relationships involved in the client's problem.

3. "Objective viewing" by the therapist was deemed the chief means of untangling relationships which might be too threatening or too symbolic for the client to cope with effectively.

4. Early life-patterns and experiences may appear again in different guise, hidden from the consciousness of the organism. This presupposed both conscious and subconscious "levels" of the mind.

5. Responsibility was held to be a pseudo-concept, since the whole pattern of a person's life was thought to be almost totally determined by factors (forces, drives, instincts, early experiences) beyond his power to alter. Freud therefore rejected absolutes, fixed moral laws, and other evidences which implied freedom of choice. If one *could not* do otherwise, reasoned Freud, "ought" becomes a meaningless term.

6. After catharsis and a logical working through of the *meanings* involved in the client's experiences, the therapist was to point out what the client might do, or lead him to see what he might do, to alleviate his suffering or at least enable him to live with his problems. The therapist was to prescribe what behavior was likely to occur and what course of action could best serve the client.

At the same time that Freud's works were becoming widely read and discussed, the vocational guidance movement in this country was getting under way. It was no accident that this new field followed the same emphasis in handling problems in vocational selection. The basic method was the same: collect all pertinent information, synthesize it, then present to the client the likely picture of what successes might follow, or not follow, if he pursued the various courses of action open to him. Although the client was free to break off the counseling relationship and to disregard the prescriptions of the vocational counselor, as a patient might choose to disregard the prescription of a medical doctor, the prescription was there.

The socio-cultural setting in which the prescriptive counseling framework arose is important. From shortly after the close of the nineteenth century until approximately 1940, American society had gone through one global war and was on the brink of another. It had weathered the Great Depression, had seen floods of immigration, had experienced rapid urban growth and problems, and had become embroiled in debates about educational philosophy and methods. The resultant personal problems, as well as intergroup and intercultural ones, were to be expected as a matter of course. Large numbers of people sought aid in coping with the problems of vocational choice and adjustment, marital difficulties, conflicts of old and new ideas, and many more. With limited psychological and social work facilities and personnel, and with the training of counselors quite limited, the listen-and-prescribe method was the most expedient, if not the most effective, way of serving. Perhaps, under the conditions, it was the only alternative, short of disregarding altogether the plight of human beings in distress.

The writings of so-called "directive" or "clinical" counselors were the most highly regarded guidelines before the 1940's; the nondirective school of thought was virtually unknown and unlabeled.

The fact that progressive education ran its course during the formative years of guidance colored the direction that counseling was to take for many years. The demand for statistical confirmation of hypotheses, the call to examine all assumptions, the stress laid upon the individual *in* society, rather than the older idea of the individual vs. society, and the many other scientific emphases of instrumentalism fell upon fertile ground; counseling was dedicated to individualizing education and vocations. The newer scientific emphasis such as the testing movement (tests of aptitudes, attitudes, mental abilities, etc.) did not call to question the prescriptive techniques; it merely gave impetus to the giving of advice, for now there were *actuarial guidelines* for the process of prescribing. Counseling could boast of objectivity and scientific aplomb.

Throughout the period when counseling was adopting the objective test method of improving predictions and prescriptions, the philosophy of instrumentalism was declaring a commitment to democracy, to individual freedom, to pursuing knowledge wherever it might lead. Such commitments seemed in keeping with the writings of early authors in the guidance movement. A society in which free choice of occupations and of life-style was an established aim was consonant with what guidance workers were trying to do. The ultimate aim of guidance was aiding people to live fuller, more fruitful lives. There was no joy in manipulating people for the sake of manipulating. The intent of it all was the happiness of the individuals and the resultant maximum harmony in the whole nation. Therefore, the stated goals of the Deweyan instrumentalists became largely the commitments of the guidance movement. One need only peruse the goals of education in the writings of the progressive educators from 1920 to 1940 and compare these with the "objectives of guidance" as set forth by any major writer in the field of guidance up to 1940 to affirm this point.

The fact that progressive education was winning acceptance at precisely the same time that counseling was coming into being and striving for formal acceptance has led some writers to the conclusion that the philosophy of guidance is instrumentalism, the prevailing philosophy of the progressive education movement. This fact of historical propinquity and the mutual cooperation and reinforcement that the one gave to the other was not identical with a cause-effect relationship. It was not the same as having identical basic presuppositions. Agreement on *objectives* is quite possible although two given groups proceed from quite different presuppositions. For example, two groups of citizens might live at approximately the same time in history (some citizens might even be members of both groups); the first group might favor the study of labor unions or some other topic as means to a greater understanding of our national history with the hope that so doing would stimulate more active, patriotic citizenship. The study of labor unions in this instance would be thought a means to the end of active, patriotic citizenship. The presupposition, whether founded or unfounded, acts as a desirable assumption to the attainment of a chosen objective. In this case the chosen objective is active, patriotic citizenship. (The test of the meaning of this is quite another matter; the criteria must be spelled out). The presupposition is that the study of labor unions is a *necessary*—although not, perhaps, a *sufficient*—condition for attaining the objective.

The second group of citizens might heartily agree with the first group that the study of labor unions should be part of the school curriculum, but for an entirely different reason. Perhaps group sentiment is that labor unions are evil, and that the study of these evil groups would discourage joining such organizations by the future workers of America. The second group would have chosen as its objective the discouragement of the joining of labor unions by tomorrow's workers. They would have presupposed that a study of labor unions is necessary to achieve this end. Both groups have agreed upon an "objective," but the presuppositions upon which they are operating are quite different. The terminology employed by either group might appear similar: "Make America Strong," "Enlighten the Citizens of Tomorrow," "Meet the Needs of Youth," and others. The two groups might aid each other without really being aware of the fundamental difference in basic presuppositions.

This is not to say that the disparity in *social aims* of the early guidance movement and those of the leaders of progressive education was so great as in the hypothetical case mentioned. Indeed, there were some large areas of basic agreement in social aims. But also there were some hard-to-reconcile differences concealed in part by the clichés, catch phrases, and similar exhortations. This chapter will indicate later a contention in the literature of guidance (arrived at three times at least by different writers) that instrumentalism has been the philosophy which best fits guidance.

The final years of the prescriptive stage in guidance served well the purpose of taking guidance out of the realm of the purely subjective, and made counselors aware that research can serve an important function in alleviating human problems of choice and adjustment. There are counselors today, according to Paterson, who operate almost entirely on the basis of test results, but these guidance workers are "arrested in their professional development." The current literature of even the most directive writers emphasizes that the individual counselee must make his own decisions. Some advice-giving is still acceptable, but the stark prescriptive quality has virtually disappeared from the literature today.

Nondirective Stage

The next major stage of development was what might be termed the nondirective or the "less directive" stage. It would not be true to the facts of guidance history to give the impression that nondirective counseling suddenly appeared and that all prescriptive or test-centered workers then closed shop. All the stages of guidance evolved from the previous ones, overlapped them, and emerged. However, the client-centered, nondirective school of thought brought about significant changes in the thinking of even the most prescriptive counselors. Perhaps one mark of any new theory is that, in its eagerness for acceptance, it "oversells" its position. This may be in part the reason for so many of the professional claims and counterclaims of the two "schools of thought" in the guidance literature during the formative years of nondirective counseling. At any rate, the new emphasis was a potent force in the evolution of a philosophical foundation for guidance.

Carl R. Rogers has been the leading spokesman for the nondirective point of view. He followed in the tradition of many philosophers and psychologists who had stressed the potentiality of the human being to solve his own problems of choice and adjustment. Basically, Rogers' approach rests upon rather simple, straightforward presuppositions. He has spelled out his basic *assumptions* quite clearly in his books on therapy (see Bibliography); however, his *presuppositions* have not been presented. It is imperative that these be made explicit, since Rogers later espoused phenomenology, and there appears to be room for serious doubt that the presuppositions of the one are those of the other. The objectives often have been stated to be identical, but even this is open to question.

It appears that Rogers has presupposed that:

1. An objective order of reality exists whether man knows much of it or not. It is one over which man has virtually no control.

2. Man can know only his phenomenal world, which Rogers views as a sort of total of all his life's forces *as perceived* by the client. (This is almost identical with Lewin's "life-space" concept.)

3. There are causal relationships in the objective physical world. Causality applies also to the world of the human psyche, but is complex and can be understood only by somehow entering the "mental and emotional skin" of the client.

4. Empathy is possible to a great extent. The extent depends upon the ability of the counselor or therapist to come to know the meanings of the client. The sharing of common objects of experience can aid in this process.

5. Each human personality seeks to maintain itself and its equilibrium in the face of constant threats from a hostile world. The personality is relatively stable, even though its exact components and the phenomenal field are constantly in flux.

6. The counselor, like all other human beings, has some values around which his life is built. These must be kept out of the counseling process as far as possible in order to avoid the danger of impressing the views of the counselor upon the client. If the ideal could be attained, there would be total absence of the counselor's values. Every human being has a right to his own life-style and his own values, but has no right to impress these upon another.

7. A democratic form of government appears to offer the type of society conducive to the value-exploration and self-determination necessary for the success of nondirective counseling. Rogers has often stated a commitment to this.

8. Every person has a right to counseling in his time of stress, but also the right to reject it or discontinue it at any time.

These appear to be the irreducible minimum of presuppositions which underlie Rogerian counseling. His basic goal has been the freedom of the individual, for he has stated often that, given the freedom to work through his problems in the presence of an unthreatening, sympathetic counselor, man can grow in the ability to solve not only an immediate problem, but also in the ability to live more fully and to learn to cope with his problems as they arise in the future.

Often the statement of Rogers' credo is taken to imply complete relativity of values. Indeed, in some passages of his work the inference would seem justified. Demonstration will be attempted herein to show that Rogers has in fact leaned toward a form of axiological realism, however. This does not in any way invalidate his major presuppositions or his methodological statements. It does, however, make difficult, if not impossible, his complete acceptance of phenomenological theory. It is proposed that Rogers' counseling procedures have much in common with those of the phenomenologists in psychology, but that the philosophical position of phenomenology contains presuppositions which Rogerians, if consistent, cannot accept. Perhaps Rogers and his followers were the pre-phenomenologists in psychology, and perhaps Rogerian thinking will give way to complete phenomenology in counseling, but the cost will be great in terms of Rogers' avowed conviction about the nature of man and the nature of human values.

Before leaving the "Rogerian influence stage" of the development of guidance, it might prove useful to examine some key statements by Rogers concerning his credo in counseling. The following are the conditions which Rogers has stated *cannot* prevail if his brand of counseling is to be most effective:

1. The component factors of the individual's adjustment are so adverse that, even with changed attitudes and insight, he could not cope with it. Destructive experiences in the family or social group, or a destructive environment, added to his own inadequacies in health,

abilities, and competencies, make adjustment very unlikely, unless the environmental setting is changed.

2. The individual is inaccessible to counseling, in that reasonable opportunity and effort fail to discover any means by which he can express his feelings and problems. (An example would be the highly withdrawn individual in the incipient stages of schizophrenic psychosis, who cannot express his obviously conflicting attitudes.)

3. Effective environmental treatment is simpler and more efficient than a direct therapeutic approach. This condition probably prevails only when the problem-creating situation is almost entirely environmental; an inadequate school curriculum, an unfortunate place of residence, an irritable and incompetent foreman, or some other factor in the environment being responsible for the problem.

4. The individual is too young or too old, too dull, or too unstable for a direct type of therapy. (See the previous sections for more exact definitions of these conditions.)[2]

From these conditions it is apparent that Rogers recognizes and presupposes the items numbered as presuppositions 1, 3, and 5, respectively, in attempting any application of his theory to therapy.

Rogers has very clearly stated the assumptions of nondirective or client-centered therapy. The following is a statement of his working assumptions:

I. Every individual exists in a continually changing world of experiences of which he is the center.

II. The organism reacts to the field as it is experienced and perceived. This perceptual field is, for the individual, reality.

III. The organism reacts as a whole to this phenomenal field.

IV. The organism has one basic tendency and striving—to actualize, maintain and enhance the experiencing organism.

V. Behavior is basically the goal-directed attempt of the organism to satisfy its needs as experienced, in the field as perceived.

VI. Emotion accompanies and in general facilitates such goal-directed behavior, the kind of emotion being related to the seeking versus the consummatory aspects of the behavior, and the intensity of the emotion being related to the perceived significance of the behavior for the maintenance and enhancement of the organism.

VII. The best vantage point for understanding behavior is from the internal frame of reference of the individual himself.

VIII. A portion of the total perceptual field gradually becomes differentiated as the self.

IX. As a result of interaction with the environment, and particularly as a result of evaluational interaction with others, the structure of self is formed—an organized, fluid, but consistent conceptual pattern of perceptions of characteristics and relationships of the "I" or the "me," together with values attached to these concepts.

X. The values attached to experiences, and the values which are a part of the self structure, in some instances are values introjected or taken over from others, but perceived in distorted fashion, as if they had been experienced directly.

XI. As experiences occur in the life of the individual, they are either (a) symbolized, perceived, and organized into some relationship to the self, (b) ignored because there is no perceived relationship to the self structure, (c) denied symbolization or given a distorted symbolization because the experience is inconsistent with the structure of the self.

XII. Most of the ways of behaving which are adopted by the organism are those which are consistent with the concept of self.

XIII. Behavior may, in some instances, be brought about by organic experiences and needs which have not been symbolized. Such behavior may be inconsistent with the structure of the self, but in such instances the behavior is not "owned" by the individual.

XIV. Psychological maladjustment exists when the organism denies to awareness significant sensory and visceral experiences, which consequently are not symbolized and organized into the gestalt of the self-structure. When this situation exists, there is a basic or potential psychological tension.

XV. Psychological adjustment exists when the concept of the self is such that all the sensory and visceral experiences of the organism are, or may be, assimilated on a symbolic level into a consistent relationship with the concept of self.

XVI. Any experience which is inconsistent with the organization or structure of self may be perceived as a threat, and the more of these perceptions there are, the more rigidly the self-structure is organized to maintain itself.

XVII. Under certain conditions, involving primarily complete absence of any threat to the self-structure, experiences which are inconsistent with it may be perceived, and examined, and the structure of self revised to assimilate and include such experiences.

XVIII. When the individual perceives and accepts into one consistent and integrated system all his sensory and visceral experiences, then he is necessarily more understanding of others and is more accepting of others as separate individuals.

XIX. As the individual perceives and accepts into his self-structure more of his organic experiences, he finds that he is replacing his present value system—based so largely upon introjections which have been distortedly symbolized—with a continuing organismic valuing process.[3]

Rogers has stated that the phenomenological model of behavior closely describes his own thinking. However, there appears to be reason to question this. It may be advisable to compare the undergirding of phenomenology with the foregoing stated assumptions of Rogers. Then we can discuss the presuppositions from which the stated assumptions stem.

Comparison: Rogers and Phenomenologists

The phenomenological model usually quoted and referred to in the literature of guidance is that expounded by Snygg and Combs. These men have clearly detailed what their view of human behavior entails. Their first assumption is a vital one in our comparison of Rogerian presuppositions with those of phenomenology.

1. Choice is a pseudo-concept. It does not occur in fact.

. . . we might say that the individual is engaged in a continuous process of making "choices." As a matter of fact, *no choice whatever* exists. He attempts that which appears to him self-enhancing and attempts to avoid that which appears to him as threatening. What he does is dependent upon the differentiations he can make in his phenomenal field. Ordinarily this process occurs with a minimum of disturbance to the organism. It is seldom clearly differentiated by the individual. Occasionally two or more differentiations may appear in the field and the individual may, himself, describe the situation as making a "choice." If we could see the situation as he saw it at the moment of his behavior we would probably discover that he made no "choice" at all but behaved as he had to behave to maintain or enhance his phenomenal self. The term "choice" is a term from an *external frame of reference* which the individual may use in describing his behavior because, when he looks at his own behavior he is making an external observation, too. As he attempts to look back at his behavior, it looks to him as though he made a "choice" just as it may have appeared to others observing his behavior.

It should be pointed out that the term "*conflict*," like "choice," is a *term of external description*. Indeed, conflict is but a form of "choice" under stress. The individual, however, does not experience conflict. He experiences threat to need satisfaction. The threat experienced is always a function of the perception as related to need satisfaction. He experiences threat to self-maintenance from one or more differentiations of his self which he is unable to accept at that moment . . . Such threatening differentiations may occur in rapid sequence and even be described by the individual as "conflict." In so doing, he is making an *external observation* of his behavior *just as any outsider would.* . . . Where inconsistent definitions of self exist in the same individual, it will usually be observed that one of these exists only at a low level of differentiation. Antagonistic concepts of self cannot exist at high levels of differentiation at the same time unless one is regarded as *not* self. This is the sort of thing which occurs in dual personalities.[4]

This quotation spells out clearly the phenomenological contentions of Snygg and Combs. Choice to them is merely the resultant action which is a direct function of the phenomenal field at a given time. The presupposition is that all behavior is determined; choice is inevitably a meaningless word in all forms of behavior. Man cannot do otherwise. He is bound by the organismic trait of self-maintenance and self-enhancement. His actions will always be those which appear to him to serve these ends. From an observer's point of view the actions might appear wholly inconsistent with serving these ends, but at the given moment the behaving organism feels that he is doing what he ought to do; indeed, he can feel no other way. Choice is a sham, a semantic deception.

If such is the case, it becomes difficult to see how Rogerians can accept such an account of human behavior and still counsel as if, in the words of Rogers, ". . . we must provide an atmosphere in which the individual can work through his problems, not under threat, and can make his own decisions in the light of clearer perspective." Really making one's own decisions is logically impossible, given the premises of Snygg and Combs.

Indeed, one can argue that, given counseling or some other restructuring of the phenomenal field, the client will perceive a situation in a different way, and will thereby react in a different (hopefully, more effective) manner, but this is begging the philosophical question. With the *new* structure of the phenomenological field, the philosophical condition is unchanged. Given the new structure, a different decision will be made, but it is not a *choice;* the actions of the organism are determined by the forces— whatever they may be—at the instant of action, as before. "Choice" is still only a word, meaning in phenomenological writings, an action one must take, if it means anything at all. It is a word devoid of any referent in experience, unless it has been applied from an external point of reference to the actions of another, and even then it is only a pseudo-concept. It is tantamount to saying only, "My own phenomenal field allows me to see two or more possibilities for his behavior; why can't he see it also?" Such description, it would seem, would be unpalatable to Rogerian counselors, since there would be no point in trying to let the individual make his own decisions! Others can restructure his field, but if they do so, they have presented the client with a phenomenal field not of his own making, and one which makes his "choice" for him. He cannot react otherwise. *Determinism* is by definition a presupposition of phenomenology. Restructing the field of the client does not change this basic fact if one is a phenomenologist, whether or not he calls himself "nondirective" and whether or not he gives lip service to "choice."

It is interesting to view this state of affairs from the behavior of the counselor as well as that of the client. If one accepts the view, as Rogers has stated he does, that a person's actions are determined at X point in time and space by his phenomenological field, then choice is a meaningless term. A counselor, then, *does what he must do* in every utterance he makes. His own need is the same as his client's: the maintenance and enhancement of the phenomenal self. Perhaps his field is larger than that of his client, and more clearly differentiated. Yet the fact remains: he makes no choice even as to the "school" of counseling he follows. His past experiences determine this—as they influence his field today, at X moment. His choices in every way are determined by his own field as he perceives it. His field changes to some degree by every utterance of the client; it is a fluid field, ever restructured; but at X point what the counselor does and says is determined by his field, just as the client's is, unless the counselor is in some unstated way unlike all others in the physical universe. He does what he must do; praise and blame for him, as for his client, is hollow.

Can a Rogerian counselor accept this phenomenological account of the counseling interview, and remain *both* a Rogerian *and* a phenomenologist? At the level of objectives, and of agreement in certain terminology, the two positions appear compatible. But at the level of presuppositions, holding both positions becomes extremely difficult and tenuous, if not impossible. Rogerians must re-examine their allegiance to phenomenology. Choice is a *keystone* to the one, a *millstone* to the other.

By way of summary, Rogerians can accept cause and effect, and many other major presuppositions of phenomenology. They can accept the major views of therapy, most of the terminology, and many commitments of the phenomenologists, but Rogerians postulate a type of "self-motivator" within the human personality. This assumption is not consonant with phenomenology. A new, more comprehensive philosophical framework appears to be needed.

Further complicating matters is that the phenomenologist *does not provide for the confirmability*—even in principle—of his hypothesis that one's phenomenal field precludes genuine "choice" and decisions. This is an important matter. From the extended quotation from Snygg and Combs previously given, this fact becomes apparent: Snygg and Combs have said in effect that "choice" is merely an external evaluation of a state of affairs which in fact is an illusion. They have stated that *if* one could view "from within the behaver's field," the action taken would be the only thing he could have done. Immediately after this statement comes the *denial* that anyone, including the subject himself, *could* do so. Even if the subject himself, who has lived through the experience and the resulting action, tried to "look back" at the action, and if he then felt that there were in fact two or more courses of action open to him, Snygg and Combs would not admit this as evidence, for they then say that after X time has passed, it cannot be re-created—even by the subject himself. To view the past action-decision moment, X, at a time *after* it, Y, is to view it from a phenomenal field which has changed; the act of introspection itself alters the field; the spatio-temporal occurrence of whatever action the client did, in fact, take alters the viewpoint and the field of the client at time Y. Such a position *precludes the testing of the hypothesis* that man's behavior is totally determined by the phenomenal field at the instant of action. It is indeed tautological. It is tantamount to saying, "Man takes the course of action that he takes." It admits of no test of confirmability; it is as much an act of sheer faith as that of any religious profession. The phenomenologists have based their whole system upon a presupposition which is unconfirmable *even in principle*.

Further, phenomenology employs a construct (*viz.*, the field of forces perceived by the actor) in explaining behavior which has no confirmable referent in experience. Such a construct, without confirmability, might in fact be the case, but to follow it blindly and without hope of verification or disproof is rather similar to professing belief in Feigl's amusing "Blue Demon" which makes his watch keep time. Admittedly no one can see the demon, no test of his presence can be made, and other things such as the interaction of the moving parts appear to make the watch operate; but it is Feigl's demon, he states with tongue in cheek, which actually makes it tick. Even if one alters the watch by removing a part or adding a part (restructuring the field?), no one can say that the "real" cause of the watch's refusal to run is not the sulking, angry reaction of the Blue Demon to such intrusion![5]

Snygg and Combs have defined psychotherapy as "the provision of experience whereby the individual is enabled to make more adequate differentiations of the phenomenal self and its relations to external reality." Together with this definition, they have specified four major problems which effective therapy must take into account:

1. Therapy must deal effectively with the problem of threat.
2. Therapy must be concerned with change in client meanings.
3. Therapy must result in the more adequate satisfaction of need.
4. More particularly, therapy must be concerned with change in the phenomenal self.[6]

These four points seem in keeping with the assumptions of Rogerian counseling, another reason perhaps for the embracing of phenomenology by those of the nondirective school.

Phenomenological Stage

As has been indicated, the nondirective stage in the development of guidance and therapy has merged gradually with the movement called phenomenology. The merging had one great advantage for guidance. The so-called split between the "nondirectives" and the "clinical counselors" in the 1940's threatened to become a serious schism detrimental to the guidance movement. The emergence of the clearly stated assumptions of phenomenology, especially those of Snygg and Combs, provided a common meeting ground, it seemed, for both schools of thought. Indeed, both schools were dedicated to helping people in the stresses of daily living; both were interested in finding a consistent group of principles from which to work; both were willing to find some common ground for reconciling their differences, if to do so would aid the profession. If one keeps in mind the stated assumptions of the nondirectives and the systematic procedures of the test-conscious clinical counselors, it will be apparent that the beliefs stated by the phenomenologists provided a kind of common ground acceptable to both. As we have already pointed out, however, many of the commonalities were at the level of similarities in terminology rather than at the bedrock presuppositional level.

We have discussed Snygg and Combs' first assumption: 1. Choice is a pseudo-concept. It does not occur in fact. To continue, paraphrasing closely the contentions of Snygg and Combs:

2. Behavior is regular and lawful.

3. The phenomenal field is the determinant of behavior.

4. Man can know only his phenomenal field.

5. There is a pre-existent reality, but man can know only that part of it which composes his phenomenal field.

6. Field perceptions at any given moment may exist at any and all levels of differentiation, from the vaguest to the sharpest.

7. The phenomenal fields of individuals are somehow connected and communication is possible.

8. Communication is the process of acquiring a greater mutual understanding of one another's phenomenal fields and can take place only when some mutual characters already exist.

9. All experiences are phenomenal in character; the fact that two individuals are in the same physical situation does not even give a relatively common experience.

10. People who share common roles in a common culture and its potentialities for common experiences inevitably develop common characteristics in their phenomenal fields and consequently in their behavior which mark them off from people of other cultures.

11. For reason 10 above, people of one culture tend to "objectify" their beliefs; these "givens" are not shared by those of other cultures, for the same reasons.

12. An individual's behavior has a one-to-one relationship with his phenomenal field; it is therefore possible to reconstruct, by inference, his phenomenal field.

13. To predict phenomenologically, one must follow two steps: Reconstruct an individual's field from his behavior, and understand how fields change.

14. The phenomenal field is always organized and meaningful, seen from the perspective of the person himself.

15. The field of any individual is both much more and less than the field which is potentially available in the immediate physical environment.

16. The phenomenal field is a product of selection, but the "selection" is carried on by the individual as a means of satisfying his needs, and in conformity with the existing organization of his phenomenal field.

17. The meaning of any situation or object is simply an awareness of the behavior that the object or the situation requires or enables him to make.

18. "Free Will" is a sham. It is an illusion seen from the restricted point of view of the behaver. An external observer sees so much evidence of causation that he must accept determinism. Prediction and control are possible only where behavior is lawful and caused.

19. At any given time the field of the given individual is organized with reference to his needs and the activity by which he is trying to satisfy them at the time.

20. Because of the great difference in the individual fields the same physical objects and events have very different significance in the fields of different individuals or in the field of the same individual at different times.

21. Memories of the past and expectations of the future will come and go as figure-ground in conformity with the needs of the individual.[7]

These were the basic tenets stated by Snygg and Combs, the working assumptions of phenomenology. Their presentation is the most widely quoted one in the literature of guidance, and could therefore be said to represent the particular brand of phenomenology which has influenced the thinking of guidance theorists. It is to this formulation that the theorists in guidance return again and again, as they examine the assumptions and philosophical problems confronting them. This is not to say that all guidance theorists embrace phenomenology; it is to say that those who have been influenced by phenomenology have, in the main, chosen the clearly presented model of Snygg and Combs. Therefore, it is to their brand of phenomenology that all comments, criticisms, and plaudits in this book are addressed.

Theorists in both the nondirective and the clinical-counseling camps have found that their particular assumptions and methods in counseling could utilize the phenomenological model. This accounts for the frequent references to phenomenology.

Phenomenology provided the nearest approximation to unified theory and philosophy that guidance has discovered thus far. However, there have been indications that the newer insights of *Dasein-analyse* psychology and philosophical outlook can encompass all these positive points while obviating some of the not so apparent, yet ever-present, difficulties which guidance wedded to phenomenology must face.

Reduced to presuppositions, phenomenology would present itself in somewhat the following manner:

1. A real world exists independent of the knower. Its existence can be inferred, but not experienced directly.

2. Reason exists and is the tool whereby inferences can be made, on the basis of past experiences.

3. Inference from past experiences in one's own phenomenal field are the only source of knowledge, other than certain "raw sensations" obtained by sensory experiences. "New" knowledge is just the re-structuring of knowns and the incorporation of what we might call *nouvelles* ("raw sensations" which become another force in one's field of forces).

4. The pre-existent world of objects and the existent world of situations follow certain predictable "laws" and can be known by reason via inference.

5. One's phenomenal field at any given instant wholly determines his behavior.

6. Naturalism is the ontological concomitant of phenomenology, and supernaturalism is excluded as nonparsimonious.[8]

7. The individual has "needs" which represent the actions necessary to maintain or enhance his phenomenal self.

The above presuppositions seem the irreducible minimum required to constitute the framework of phenomenology. Nothing has been said of values or of axiological presuppositions, since it follows from presuppositions 5, 6, and 7 that one will choose (value) those objects and acts which will maintain or enhance his phenomenal self, or, more properly, one will choose those acts or objects as "of value" which at a given time X with the then-existent phenomenal structure Y seem from *his* point of view to enhance or maintain his phenomenal self. Values, then, are an extension of one's phenomenal self. What is valuable or valued by one person may not, need not, be valued by another, or even by the same person at time Z.

The above statement of "individual valuing" inherent in phenomenology leaves unanswered the question of whether there are *some* (transcendent) values which are at all times valued by all men, the "absolutes" of traditional philosophy. *If* a given value, X, could be demonstrated in thousands of cases, or in millions of cases, to recur as "chosen" by men of various cultures and in various walks of life, then a case might be built for X as a "perennial" value. But even in this case, the rejection of that given value by *one man* would cast doubt upon its genuine universal character. Perhaps the best that could be said of such a value, if indeed one could be identified at all, is that it represents the fulfillment of some need in the phenomenal selves of the experiencing individuals, although it would be quite another matter to demonstrate *what* need it fulfilled in each individual case! The existence of eternal values breaks down under its own weight under phenomenology. Given a particular culture with many common objects of understanding and "communication-potential" (as mentioned in Snygg and Combs' work and described under points 8, 10, and 11 on page 71 of this study), certain values will perhaps be "objectified"—law is an example of this, as is custom and taboo—and come to be regarded as sacrosanct or absolute, but this does not mean more than that this action or custom has in the past, and will in the foreseeable future, have the effect of enhancing or maintaining the phenomenal selves of *most* of the people of that culture. To confirm that the law is addressed to the enhancement of those *of* a culture as opposed to those *not of* that culture, one need only be referred to the omnipresent immigration laws, restrictive trade treaties among nations, and other culture-perpetuating and enhancing measures. Herein is macrocosmic manifestation of the phenomenal self; those who share many features in their phenomenal fields present a united front against those who do not, or against those they feel do not share their needs and aspirations or goals. It is the same in principle as the actions of the individual (microcosmic manifestation) to protect his goals against other individuals. If the old "evidence" of ontogeny's recapitulation of phylogeny were admitted today as "strengthening" a theory, phenomenology would indeed have strong support.

Phenomenology has been quite consistent in its methods and statement of theory. If one has granted the seven presuppositions from which it proceeds, then what follows is quite to be expected and is a very compelling system of dealing with and explaining human behavior. There are a few points which need explication, however.

Snygg and Combs made a haunting statement in their *Individual Behavior.* "We are not always able to remember what we need, but we do need what we remember." [9] A moment's reflection will point up the importance of that statement for the theory of phenomenology. If the phenomenological philosophy of human behavior states that man "chooses" from his necessity to fulfill a need, why does he not choose to remember "what he needs"? If to remember X would enhance or maintain one's phenomenal self, it would follow from phenomenological theory that one would remember X. If the first half of the above quoted statement is true, then phenomenology owes an explanation of what prevents or blocks the remembering which would enhance or maintain self. One finds, following the cryptic observation, an explanation centering upon the postulation that what is "forgotten" means that other more important items have become "figure," and that what is "forgotten" has simply become "ground" and therefore is not immediately able to influence the field (i.e., is temporarily "out" of the field). To reason in this way appears question-begging and tautological. If one needs to remember something and cannot do so—even when the basic hypothesis of phenomenology indicates that he *must* (determined) do so—it appears illegitimate to say, "Well, you see, he needs something else *more.*" This is tantamount to saying, "He needs what he chooses (remembers), and chooses what he needs." The reasoning is circular. It offers no confirmable evidence for its assumption. Perhaps the original statement by Snygg and Combs ought to read, "We need what we remember; if we do not remember something, it is not needed strongly enough." Such a statement might be more in keeping with the presuppositions of the system.

"Change"

Also in need of explication is a reflection on another page of the Snygg and Combs' [10] work mentioned above. They have made the point in question quite clear at several points in their books, but writers in the field of guidance have seized upon the "fluidity of the phenomenal field" as synonymous with Dewey's "change" and have on this basis ascribed to Deweyan instrumentalism the position of "the" guidance philosophy. Guidance writers have then embraced phenomenology as a sort of method by which Dewey's philosophy could serve guidance. "Change" to the phenomenologist is quite different from Dewey's concept of change. In fact, the meticulous phenomenologist has hesitated to use the word "change." Snygg and Combs remarked:

> It is quite true that figure is constantly dropping back into ground where it is "forgotten" and loses its potency in determining behavior, but this lapse into ground is not an independent process but is the necessary complement of the emergence of other features into figure. Since it is the newly emerged figure which has the major influence on behavior at the moment *it seems better to emphasize the emergent aspect of the process and call it "differentiation" rather than just "change."* [11] [Italics mine.]

From the above it can be seen that change was not viewed as the sudden passing of a happening, an irrevocable disappearing from being, but rather was the centering of attention on other matters which satisfied more immediate needs. It was not a matter of "losing" something, but of relegating it to the fringes ("ground") of experience, where it was, in principle at least, available to serve future needs. This was strongly reminiscent of Locke's physio-psychological dictum that the *tabula rasa* contains all experiences, that none are ever wiped off, but only "buried," so to speak, under others which serve the present needs better. This stratagem on the part of the phenomenologists was consistent with the teaching that the need of the individual determines his actions, and that choice is a sham; it also obviated the necessity of explaining where a memory goes if it can never be recalled again. The phenomenologists have offered no proof that his "to the fringes" explanation is valid, but it is at least logically consistent with the rest of his theory of behavior.

The point of the foregoing three paragraphs is that one must tread lightly when embracing both instrumentalism and phenomenology on the basis of concepts which seem to be alike. A more valid means of ascertaining whether they are compatible or identical is through the examination of the presuppositions of each.

The Philosophical Position of Modern Guidance

In the matter of determining a philosophical position for guidance among the known schools of thought, it would seem that a form of realism, rather than experimentalism, would best fit the stated and implied beliefs of the writers in guidance. This statement will be discussed later in this chapter.

The statement made in the preceding paragraph referred, of course, to the ideas already in the guidance literature: to the commitments made, the concepts accepted, the postulates and constructs used, the statements of credo and their justifications, the criteria acceptable as proof, the emphases of the research done, the stated aims, and the ethical assumptions. If realism of a particular sort seems to fit best what has been and to a large degree what is the philosophy of guidance, it appears that such a realism is merging into a new framework, one which will be more suitable for the challenges of today and tomorrow. It is proposed that the realism which has served guidance so well in the recent past must give way, and is doing so, to a more comprehensive philosophy. There are several strong indications of inadequacies within the present philosophical framework. All writers who have given these indications have moved toward the tenets of a European movement in therapy called *Daseinanalyse*. The orientation of *Daseinanalyse* is so vital to the future of guidance in America that if only *one point* could be made in this book, it would be that those charged with the training of counselors in America ought to read with extreme care the *Daseinanalyse* thinking concerning what therapy is and can do. With thoughtful application, *Daseinanalyse* and the philosophy behind it can be of service not only to therapy, but to all phases of guidance. Counselor-educators might then lay down guidelines for the future orientation of counselors. A beginning in this direction is shown in Chapter Four of this study. The presuppositions of *Daseinanalyse* have been presented for critical evaluation by those who give direction to the field of guidance. If the assumptions of this study are substantially correct, *Daseinanalyse* will far overshadow the realism which at present seems to describe the practices and theories of guidance, and will provide courageous guidelines for the future of guidance. It says what every dedicated counselor has known in his deepest feelings, and what the novice counselor must learn to become more than superficially effective. The writings of certain *Daseinanalyse* therapists are to guidance what Pestalozzi's writings were to education. They postulate a certain outlook on mankind without which very little really meaningful counseling can take place. Just as Pestalozzi stated that without the characteristic of "love" (specially defined by him) one cannot really be a teacher, so without the deepest understanding of what counseling is and can be, one cannot counsel better than superficially.

Common "Principles" or "Assumptions" in Guidance: Realism

To be discussed are the presuppositions upon which guidance has operated up to 1950, the date of Cribbin's doctoral study. Cribbin identified the following common principles or assumptions in over two hundred guidance texts from 1935 to 1950. These fundamental assumptions, from which presuppositions will be deduced, have not changed substantially since 1950. The minor alterations which have taken place will be noted, but only if they have influenced the presuppositional structure.

1. Guidance is based on the recognition of the dignity and worth of the individual and on his right to personal assistance in time of need.

2. Guidance is student-centered, being concerned for the optimum development of the whole student and the fullest realization of his potentialities for individual and social ends.

3. Guidance, as a point of view, is as old as good education. It is modern with reference to (a) the areas of the student's life which are considered to be the responsibility of the school, (b) the services which it offers students, and (c) the techniques it employs to obtain its objectives.

4. Guidance is a continuous, sequential, educational process. Hence it is an integral part of education and not a mere peripheral adjunct.

5. Guidance has a responsibility to society as well as to the individual.

6. Guidance must respect the right of every student to the help and services it offers.

7. Guidance is oriented about cooperation, not compulsion. Hence, it is monitory in character with no place for coercion.

8. Guidance applies assistance given students in making wise choices, plans, interpretations, and adjustments in the critical situations of life.

9. Guidance demands a comprehensive study of the student in his cultural setting by the use of every scientific technique available. Student understanding must precede student assistance.

10. Guidance should be entrusted only to those who are naturally endowed for the task and have the necessary training and experience.

11. Guidance is the prerogative of no special clique of specialists. It requires the cooperation of all, each working within his own area of responsibility and at the level of his own competence.

12. The focus of guidance is on helping the student realize and actualize his best self rather than on solving isolated problems, be they those of the individual or the school.

13. Guidance is the mediating agency between the student and the mass of education.

14. Guidance is the individualizing, the personalizing, and the socializing element in education.

15. The guidance program must be under constant, scientific evaluation in terms of its effectiveness.[12]

No one has seriously challenged Cribbin's listing, although his evaluation of what the listing meant could be debated. One phase of Cribbin's summary of the 1935-1950 literature of guidance is of special importance here. He divides the professed aims and goals of the literature into two classes, ultimate aims and proximate aims:

Ultimate Aims

1. Best development of the individual
2. Well-rounded
3. Optimum
4. Full and balanced
5. Broad gauged
6. Physically, intellectually, emotionally, socially and spiritually. . . .
7. Self-guidance growth and growth in individual maturity
8. Self-supporting, self-contained, self-directing, and replete with inner resourcefulness
9. Individual happiness and social efficiency
10. . . . learn to live better lives

Proximate Aims

1. Develop student initiative, responsibility, self-direction, and self-guidance.
2. Develop ability to choose student's own goals wisely.
3. Know oneself, know the school, and be known by the school.
4. Anticipation, avoidance, and prevention of crises from arising in the lives of students.
5. Help the student adjust satisfactorily to school and to life.
6. Help student recognize, understand, meet and solve his problems.

7. Assist student in making wise choices, plans, and interpretations at critical points in his life.

8. Help student acquire the insights and techniques necessary to enable him to solve his own future problems.

9. Assist teachers to teach more effectively.

10. Help administrators administer more efficiently by making a maximum contribution to the total school program.

11. Develop citizens who will participate in and contribute to the democratic way of life.

12. Miscellaneous objectives: assisting the home, helping community building ethical character, fostering better human relations, and aiding international understanding.[13]

Since 1950 Cribbin's list, if extended, would have included only a few other emphases. Under the listing of common principles or assumptions, one would now perhaps include as point 16: Guidance accepts phenomenology as its *major* model of human behavior. The last point would be: 17. To some degree, guidance must serve the function of conservation of talent for national defense. However, point 17 would be controversial, with most of the controversy predicated on the words "*some degree.*" By acceptance of federal funds for the training of counselors, guidance has given at least tacit assent to the *aims* of the acts providing such funds. Thoughtful consideration of the impact of this "conservation of talent" upon individuals may result in varying shades of approval or disapproval. However, for whatever reasons, guidance has accepted the funds and thereby, to some degree at least, the aims of the acts providing the funds.

Under Cribbin's list of Ultimate Aims there would be no important additions, but the *tone* of the literature since 1950 has stressed the inner satisfactions of the client rather than outward manifestations, such as "well-roundedness," which were more prevalent in the 1940's. This was perhaps due in part to the warnings of Whyte, Riesman, Fromm, Jacob, and others who have made guidance and the general public conscious of the dangers of conformity in a free society. The commitment to democracy as a way of life was perhaps overlooked by Cribbin, or intentionally left out as "immaterial" under Ultimate Aims, but perhaps should now be included in such a listing. Individual freedom in society is a commitment which follows from Rogerian hypotheses.

It was in the matter of proximate aims that Cribbin's list appeared dated by the recent developments in guidance. These too were a result of the wide acceptance of phenomenology as a model of human behavior by the leaders in the field of guidance. Cribbin's proximate aims numbered 1, 2, 3, 4, 5, 6, 9, 10, and perhaps 11 were still often repeated in the literature, although 11 has been called to question by the recent *Daseinanalyse* developments. Points 7 and 8 appeared to have undergone severe reappraisal. Those who have accepted the phenomenological model must, if consistent, make it clear that the student does not "choose" in the traditional meaning of the word; the resultant action of what was once called a "choice situation" is determined by the "field of forces" or the "phenomenal field" at the time of the so-called "choice." Choice is not a fact, but rather an illusion seen from the point of view of the person acting. It is wholly determined, as has been herein illustrated in previous sections of this chapter.

Point 8 would not, under phenomenology, read that the counselor should "Help student acquire insights . . . to solve his own problems," but rather might read: ". . . Restructure the phenomenal field of the client so that optimum action might result." This latter point might sound overly manipulative, but it is the result of the acceptance of a completely deterministic philosophy such as phenomenology. The debate previously mentioned (in Chapter Two) between Rogers and Skinner is a pseudo-disagreement. If both men are honest and thoughtful about the consequences of their philosophies, they must agree that all guidance is manipulative; Rogers merely wants to manipulate the counseling situation to protect personal liberty, while Skinner represents efficiency in attaining a given goal, whatever goal society chooses. Rogers' phenomenology is no less manipulative than that of Skinner's behaviorism. *If* "choice" is wholly determined by the phenomenal field or phenomenal self as Snygg and Combs have repeatedly asserted (and Rogers, by his identification with their particular brand of phenomenology, has affirmed), indeed the *only way* to change "choice" in *any direction* is by restructuring the field, i.e., through manipulation, by whatever euphemism it is called.

Presuppositions from Guidance Literature

Using as a composite the work of Cribbin and the amendments to his work mentioned in the last few pages plus the literature indicated in Chapter Two of this study, the following presuppositions appear warranted:

1. An objective order of physical reality exists and affects individual existences. It exists independent of the knower.

2. Causality in the case of (physical world) objects appears to be an unquestioned fact of existence. One event follows another in time (both space and time are presupposed, also, but not explored in the literature), and the appearance of event A, if followed by event B *may* be the cause of B. This is the necessary, though not the sufficient, condition for application of the expression "A caused B." There are several possibilities in this argument which have not been set out in detail in the guidance literature, but which must not be taken lightly. *Post hoc ergo propter hoc* reasoning has long been the bane of those studying human behavior only superficially. The fact that one event precedes another does not establish cause and effect. A might be a prearranged *signal* for someone or something to cause B; A might in fact be the sole cause of B; A might be only *one* necessary factor in bringing about the occurrence of B, needing others to complete the causation; A might be only one of several factors which could cause B, singly; also possible is the fact that A is a side-product of the causal process, always occurring before B, but not contributing to its causation; or A might just possibly be present by chance in several situations. This latter possibility is easy to rule out under carefully controlled laboratory experiments, but all too often the *a priori* assumption that A is a causal factor blinds a theorist or practitioner to the non-causality relationship. This is one reason for so much superstition, time-consuming ritual, and superfluous procedure in some behavioral sciences today.

3. Each human organism has an organization of potentialities and characteristics which remain relatively stable throughout life.

4. Man can know only what is inside his phenomenal field; even inferences are made on the basis of what is in the field.

5. Client understanding precedes assisting one in the counseling relationship. (Even in catharsis, the fact that it is *permitted* and encouraged is indicative of the understanding that this is beneficial in setting the stage for therapy.)

6. Causality is accepted in personal-meanings and life-style, as well as in physical phenomena, but is a function of organismic potentialities and organizational qualities; what sets off a given reaction in one human organism might affect another quite differently. (As Snygg and Combs have pointed out, this does not mean the death knell for stimulus-response models, but does mean that somehow the organism "chooses"—or has chosen for it—the stimulus to which it will react.)
Causality is complex, but can be understood, in the human organism,

since there is a one-to-one relationship between behavior and the phenomenal field which brings it about.

7. Determinism is accepted as the framework of nature and of man's behavior. Prediction requires lawfulness and determination; man has found enough lawfulness to infer more. The alternative is too much to face.

8. Each organism has the potential to resolve his own life conflicts if only the obstacles to seeing them "objectively" (i.e., restructuring the phenomenal field) can be removed. Note, however, the Rogerian cautions on page 64 in the use of therapy with certain types of individuals such as mentally deficient, withdrawn, "environment-trapped," and others; the presupposition does not indicate that *methods* of bringing out the potentials in these types at this time, although Rogers states the hope perhaps unsupported by evidence, that such may happen.

9. The responsibility of each organism for his ultimate choices is inherent in all systems of guidance thus far conceived. This responsibility doctrine seems tenuous in view of item 7 above, but can be reconciled. Phenomenology cannot do it; *Daseinanalyse* can, as will be seen in Chapter Four.

10. The dignity and worth of the individual, and his right to pursue his own life-style is presupposed. His right to assistance in his time of need (when obstacles block his view of "true relationships") is uncontested, but his *obligation* to receive such aid is debated.

11. Guidance is concerned with the "optimum development" of each man's (presupposed) potentialities. Existentialist or *Daseinanalyse* counselors raise the question of "which potentialities and toward the end chosen by whom?"

12. The total life-space of the individual must be viewed in working with any single segment of it; the organism reacts as a whole.

13. "Change" as described in the counseling literature does not refer to Heraclitean change, an ontological and irreversible change, but rather to dynamic relationships with the objective world. Stability is a relative term, but describes the majority, if not all, of human personalities. It is interesting that "unstable" is the term used for unhealthy personalities.
As has been indicated earlier, those who have done the major theory formulation prefer the word "differentiation" or "figure-to-ground" (which implies a reversible process) rather than "change" (which implies finality and irreversibility).

14. Inferences made on the basis of past experience are a useful tool in establishing predictions in a lawful (presupposed) "closed system" universe.

15. Inference and sense perceptions are the only sources of knowledge. "New" knowledge is the restructuring of knowns and the incorporation of influences or predictions.

16. "Intuition" as a knowledge source is referred to in the literature from time to time, but can be explained in naturalistic terms, following the principle of parsimony, by reference to "vague closure," "imperfectly formed hypotheses" and other terms drawn from Gestalt psychology. There is no indication that knowledge proceeds from any source except inference from past experiences.

17. Naturalism is the ontological concomitant of phenomenology, and supernaturalism is excluded as nonparsimonious.

18. The individual has "needs" which represent the actions necessary to maintain and/or enhance his phenomenal self. (The "needs" have not been classified. It is evidently assumed that any "call to action" from the phenomenological point of view implies a "need." For the sake of semantic clarity, this word will be discussed. However, the adamant phenomenologist can still insist that *if* and *when* one acts, it is in response to a "need." It is hereby proposed that this is tautological.)

19. Freeing the individual to make his own "choices" has been proposed frequently, but this is an anomaly under phenomenology. More properly stated, this presupposition would read "Restructure the field of the client who comes for help, so that his backlog of attitudes and means for handling future problems will grow."

20. Any means of studying the student and thereby enabling the counselor to restructure the field in the direction of the client's goals is permissible, *if* such method does not infringe upon other areas of his life which he values more than the goals under discussion.

21. There are certain optimum ways of behaving which society (collective term for all individual organisms with their own potentialities) approves of as preserving itself, keeping "social equilibrium" intact. This is fundamentally a macrocosmic version of the individual behavior model of phenomenology. A reasoning organism can come to know these ways of behaving and most organisms will accept them if they are freed to see them by the removal of "barriers" which block them. There are many blocks to this congruence between the "best ways" and a given organism's view of the "best way" to live. There is no necessary conflict here between the ideal of freedom and the attempt to "get others to see the 'best solution,'" so long as no compulsion is used, and so long as the individual in question realizes a phenomenological need through a proposed course of action, or if the acceptance of this course of action will produce more "units" of freedom in the long run. But the choice must rest with the client (again, the word "choice" becomes a source of deception in phenomenological literature).

It may be noted that the presupposition just discussed does not sound at all reminiscent of Rogerian credo. Yet it must be pointed out that Rogers had hinted at this presupposition in his earlier works, and has not revised it to date. Guidance writers, especially the theistically oriented ones, may disagree as to what these values or ways of behaving are and what the *source* of the values may be, but whether they are arrived at by working consensus, religious revelation, eternal verities from race experience, or whatever, all present systems of counseling move toward some set of values, or at least admit that all persons do have values unto themselves which frequently can be generalized into codes of conduct which others share.

Rogers' Views

Rogers has stated it thus, in describing the personality which has developed optimally:

> This chapter has endeavored to present a theory of personality which is consistent with our experience and research in client-centered (non-directive) therapy. *This theory is basically phenomenological* in character, and relies heavily upon the concept of the self as an explanatory construct. It pictures the end-point of personality development as being a *basic congruence* between the phenomenal field of experience and the conceptual structure of the self—a situation which, if achieved, would represent the maximum in realistically oriented adaptation; which would mean the establishment of an individualized [individually arrived-at] value system *having considerable identity with the value system of any other equally well-adjusted* member of the human race.[14] [Italics mine.]

Thus Rogers spoke out for a correspondence theory of truth; his was a matching of individual human values with those of "race experience." If the barriers to "seeing the values that exist" (and are held by others) are removed, man will *make congruent his views* of the world and of values with what *is*. There is no clearer statement of axiological realism than this in the counseling literature. There is no clearer picture of realist epistemology than this "congruence" goal. But one example is not enough to represent a field so diverse and large as modern guidance.

Among the other writers who have given serious consideration and no little time and space to the philosophy of counseling and guidance are Williamson, Wrenn, Mathewson, and Shoben. Perhaps representative statements from these men will provide the major proof of the contention that realism of a particular sort is the present philosophical position of guidance.

MATHEWSON'S VIEWS

Mathewson stated as the "ultimate concern" of guidance:

> Optimum development and realization of the individual self, consistent with *universally valid* social obligations, moral values, and spiritual ideals.[15]

Later in the same chapter of his book, Mathewson again stated the position that pre-existent values must be taken into account, and that adjustment to these (congruence or close correspondence) was a necessity for the well-adjusted person. As a "fundamental proposition" he stated:

> The individual should be guided and educated to *adjust* creatively to social realities in the light of *moral and spiritual* values.[16]

Mathewson hinted at a pre-existent order, although this is inconsistent, unless modified, with phenomenological presuppositions:

> Man is much *more than a part of nature* in the materialistic sense. He partakes of higher forms of nature and as an intelligent *spiritual* being is able to evaluate himself and events, to form his purposes, to *receive intuitions,* to make choices and decisions.[17]

Again he stated:

> To discard the theoretical-scientific approach would mean a retrogression into a purely subjective, mystical, and irrational view of the world and of personality. On the other hand, to discard the *intuitive-artistic* view of life might tend to relegate man to the position of a *determinable unit in a mechanistic world* [this is the pivotal *basis* upon which phenomenology rests], to remove his dignity, his sense of freedom, and his feeling of responsibility.[18]

Mathewson's credo moved still further toward striving for "correspondence" with a pre-existent system:

> While holding the view that *universal events are ultimately determined by Divine Will*, we cannot escape the fact that one important determinant of the *immediate social process* is man himself.[19]

From the foregoing quotations (with all italics mine) which were typical of many others that could be cited to support Mathewson's views, it became apparent that phenomenology would *not* answer his credo; it was not the system for him, since his presuppositions precluded belief in those of Snygg and Combs, and those of other well-known phenomenologists. He presupposed:

1. A closed system universe designed by a Divine Will and working out a preconceived plan
2. A supernatural order which man can experience directly (intuition) or by inference from experience
3. Man as a creature of choice, even though the ultimate Grand Plan is predetermined by the Supernatural. Man can make choices which determine in part his own life. These are real choices, not appearances.
4. A mechanistic order of objects, a naturalistic one, in which man must move and live, but at least part of man's nature is "spiritual" and beyond naturalism
5. The existence of universals or absolutes which man can come to see and to react in accordance with. These are universally valid, not culturally determined in any sense. In that man sees and responds positively to these, he is "good." This is the correspondence theory of truth and of values. The mind-plus-body naturalism and metanaturalism dichotomy plus the correspondence theory of validation indicates *not* pragmatism, *not* phenomonology, but a form of realism as has been contended in this chapter.

That Mathewson considers pragmatism inadequate and not descriptive of his thinking is explicitly stated:

> All values cannot be judged by short-term consequences in limited settings. Thus pragmatism or *instrumentalism* by itself *does not seem* to provide a fundamentally adequate philosophy. Nor can "scientific rationalism" supply a sufficiently comprehensive view.[20]

Mathewson shared with the phenomenologists their basic assumption that man reacts only to his phenomenal field as he experiences it; he felt that modifying the field is desirable *if* so doing allows the individual to see a wider range of possibilities. But his basic tenet that man has within himself a "self-determining," direction-setting potential separated him from phenomenology, as did his insistence on supernatural design and a Divine Will as necessary presuppositions.

Mathewson's design for guidance, or, as he termed it, his "strategy," had much in common with other leaders in the field, chiefly with Wrenn. Both men have been followers of phenomenology and have seen in it great possibilities for the understanding of human behavior and the alleviation of human distress. Wrenn's presuppositions appeared to be quite similar to Mathewson's. Both men came closer to a form of realism than to either phenomenology or pragmatism, as will be demonstrated, but both indicated that their deepest feelings must seek a *form* of realism which approaches a more comprehensive philosophy. *Daseinanalyse* theory appears to answer the deepest commitments of both men.

WRENN'S VIEWS

Wrenn examined his own feelings and meanings in attempting to arrive at a philosophy of guidance and personnel work.[21] The fact that he has professed an eclectic position as a result of this, and that he has stated that instrumentalism seemed to come closest to describing the basic framework in which guidance-personnel work takes place to the contrary, it is proposed that *Daseinanalyse* philosophy and psychology follows most closely from his presuppositions. He has stated that existentialism would appeal to him "if the barriers were down." Wrenn has stated, for example, that he believes in God, a designer of the lawful universe; that he believes in the integrity of each man's personality, mercy which goes beyond the facts, and love as a positive quality of existence. He feels that these are "of the essence" of man's existence. He then indicates that the fact of major importance in regard to these values is that they permeate the spiritual phases of man's world, "whether their origin is of God, of man's experience alone, or of man's experience with God."

He expressed the tentative belief that perhaps some values are fixed, and that others change; the inconsistency of this stirs some concern. If incorporated into *Daseinanalyse* thinking, the inconsistency is explainable and able to be fit into the theory of values.

Wrenn's statement regarding the epistemology was a bit confusing.

> Since whatever is known must be known by the mind of man, then *reality is affected* by the changing knower.[22]

The conclusion does not follow from the premise. The *knower* (his phenomenal field, field of forces, or whatever his total experience may be termed) is affected by knowledge, but the *object remains uninfluenced* by the *act* of perception. The act of perceiving can perhaps set into motion certain actions on the part of the observer which will result in a change in the object's physical condition, perhaps, but the *act* of cognition does not change the nature of the object of cognition.

This quotation, too, leads in the direction of *Daseinanalyse*.

> Our totality of religious and cultural experiences has left us with a deep feeling of some eternal verities that exist in the world of man and God. For some of us, some or a part of these have their origin in the nature of God; for others they are simply ethical and humanistic concepts. For both groups, they exist as realities; they are values.

Wrenn spoke of "growth and process," rather than of "fixed products." His statements to the effect that "values grow out of experience," that a monism or wholeness of the personality is a basic assumption, that guidance accepts "what works," and that guidance modifies method on the basis of results obtained, indicate a type of realism which, coupled with his other previous statements, points all the more strongly toward the *Daseinanalyse* model.

Wrenn presupposes—if this account is typical of his other writings, and it is felt that it is—a world view which could be stated as follows:

1. There is an objective order of reality which man can come to know only to a degree because he is finite.
2. Man reacts only to what is within his phenomenal field. This field can be restructured in many ways, only one of which is through new "forces" introduced by counseling.
3. There are certain vital values in the life of every man, many of which are shared by men almost universally. The source of these values is indeterminate thus far.
4. Man is an emergent figure, since his field is constantly being restructured via experiences. His nature is not fixed.
5. The universe is a framework of system; it can never be known completely because of the emergent character of it, but man has found enough evidences of system to seek more.
6. Inference from past experiences is man's chief tool of knowing.
7. Man's feeling for his fellows is a generic positive feeling, origin not definitely known.
8. Man shares some values with his fellows; he has others which are uniquely his own.

This last statement was not contradictory nor was it a statement which was incongruous with the other sections of Wrenn's philosophy. It follows from the belief that there is an objective order of physical objects common at least in part to all men; this constituted one aspect of their phenomenal totality. Also, men tend to form societies and subcultures; in so doing they come in contact with the characteristic ways of their fellows, and accept some of their ways of viewing situations (valuing). Man's own heredity, past experiences, and present field determine how much of total reality he can see, and how he responds to it.

Wrenn's own often-professed approval of the use of tests as one more way of getting to know about the client indicated a belief in the power of knowledge through inference. Wrenn did not reify the separate "traits" (a term which has passed into ill repute in guidance because of reification in the past), but rather treated them as indicators of potentialities. This mode of thinking is a shared position of the realist and the experimentalist; but viewed in the light of Wrenn's other beliefs, it indicates that neither of these two philosophies is comprehensive or flexible enough to be his philosophy in any vital sense acceptable to him.

It would appear from the total picture of Wrenn's philosophy, derived from this and other writings, that his overriding presupposition in regard to reality may be stated as follows:

There exists a world of objects in lawful relationship to each other. These relationships change, but remain comparatively stable throughout the lifetime of any given man. Men, because of their own finiteness and their own phenomenal fields (still relatively stable yet fluctuating, and being constantly restructured by degrees) can suddenly come to view the relationships in a different manner (cf. the geocentric vs. the heliocentric theories), but this in no way changes the object of cognition. It perhaps changes the meaning it has for the man, but the object is oblivious to the change. The seeming exception to this, of course, would be the case in which the object of cognition is a *person*, who is obviously not unaffected by a new acquaintanceship, however casual. This situation, however, is totally consistent with Wrenn's outlook. The fact that the object of cognition (a second person) also has a phenomenal field which is restructured to greater or lesser degree makes no fundamental change in relatively stable properties of that individual (hair color, eyes, height, weight, language spoken) per se (i.e., solely by the action of cognition). If, however, factors other than cognition enter the situation, then changes may take place—but these take place because of a restructuring inside the phenomenal field. If, for example, a young woman falls in love with a man who admires trait X (e.g., blond hair, clear diction and correct usage, or some other trait), the woman might move in the direction of the desired trait if she feels it will enhance or maintain the relationship. Counselors see examples of this every day in their work. But it is clearly a complex of factors (emotional, past experiences, affectional needs), not the simple act of cognition, which brings about the restructuring.

Wrenn's writings revealed a respect for the "case history" as one important means of discovering "situational" meanings which a person might hold. This is another example of how inference from past experiences plays an important part in Wrenn's theory of knowledge. Wrenn has stated many times that any given situation (e.g., a broken home) is viewed differently by each individual who is exposed to the situation. If one couples the presupposition that reality exists and can be known rather completely by a given person with the presupposition that past meanings set the stage for the present ones, he arrives at a philosophical position (indicated, but of course not determined wholly by the two presuppositions) approximating a type of realism.

Wrenn's views seem to picture the situation thus: A situation X occurs—any event, such as the sound of a bell in a first grade. The new child in the school is at first only startled by the sudden noise. His view of reality in relationship to the bell is incomplete. If the other students begin to move toward the door, and if the teacher is apparently in a hurry to shoo them out, he gets the meaning, "Bell means move out." This is still an incomplete picture of the total reality of the situation. When finally he goes outside with the others and sees firemen walking about, his view of the situation is wider, but still confused. He has not seen total reality in this situation. If someone then whispers to him that this is a fire drill, and explains what that means, he is then quite close to the "'reality" of the situation. His "congruence with reality" as it exists prior to his knowledge of it, the ever-approaching "correspondence with truth" is never exactly the same as that of others, because of the individual past experiences of each child and situational differences.

When the fire-drill bell rings the next time, the objective meaning will be clear; the personal meaning will vary with the phenomenal field of a given student; to one, it may mean welcome relief from the droning of a disliked teacher, to another it may represent welcome exercise in the midst of a long arithmetic test, to still another it might mean an interruption just as he was "getting" a difficult problem on the same arithmetic test, to still another it might have some traumatic meaning because a dearly loved playmate died in a fire some years ago (and this feeling may not even be on the conscious level).

The point of all this is that one makes inferences *on the basis of his present state of knowledge*. This is all he can do. Even deduction is the result of a "present state of knowledge" preceding it. As he corrects previous inferences (less correspondent views of a relatively stable reality) he moves closer to seeing it as it really is. He can never see it totally—in all its aspects—for man is finite and exists in time and space (for example, he cannot possibly see all the firemen, for some may be on the other side of the building). The hope in guidance is that a client can see enough of reality to grasp its *essential* meaning; and this word "essential" is deliberately chosen. For Wrenn as for others who will soon be discussed, *existence precedes* essence, it appears. *Personal meanings* determine the "essence" of a situation in the only way a given man can know it. Wrenn is more concerned with these personal meanings as he encounters the personal problems of counseling and guidance than he is with the unchanged (because of cognition alone) "reality" which *exists* the same for all, but is much more (essence determined by the person). This is not the death knell for objective measurement, for this objective testing of reality in commonly understood terms is a check against total misunderstanding of personal meanings; it is merely, as Wrenn's writings make clear, an indication of what the personal meanings *probably* are (again, inference).

Thus far the premises of Wrenn fit rather well the basic postulates of phenomenology, but Wrenn has granted a particular presupposition in his personal meanings that does not coincide with the basic assumptions of phenomenology. Wrenn presupposed a God, or at least a Creating, Design-making Force. Phenomenology has admitted of no such possibility. Wrenn's superimposing of this basic presupposition is not easily accommodated by phenomenology, if it can at all, tenuously, be accommodated. The total picture of

Wrenn's own thinking is more in keeping with *Dasein* philosophy and psychology.

Rationale for This Presentation of "Representative Philosophies"

The reason for the presentation of an analysis of phenomenological presuppositions, Rogerian presuppositions and those of Mathewson and Wrenn must be made explicit. Other leading figures in guidance could have been chosen. The men chosen represent the basic positions held by almost all the others in the field. Of the major writers, only Williamson and Bordin appeared to show features which did not follow the basic thinking of these positions, and even they differed only in degree on the counseling continuum, not in kind. The men chosen, as educators of counselors, and as respected writers in the guidance literature which is widely read by other counselor-educators and counselors-in-practice, have played a great part in "restructuring the fields" (to employ the phenomenological explanation) of the people who perform the functions of guidance. It is believed that their philosophical presuppositions have been those of the great majority of the workers in the field, whether those workers have thought through these or not.

Several influences, as indicated here and in Chapter Two, may lead many to feel that neither phenomenology with its determinism, nor instrumentalism with its appealing "pursue what works" cast (an oversimplification) but with a relativity of values which shakes the inner feelings of many counselors (who often may be middle-class oriented), is the position exemplified by the lives and works of counselors. The concern of the present chapter is to point out what the recent writings have *presupposed*. The major task lies in Chapter Four. What does the most recent literature indicate for the future of guidance? A philosophy for the future will be proposed— not as a personal predilection of the investigator, but as indicated by the *presuppositions* of the literature and their meaning in our society at this time. It seems a strangely compelling philosophy; it forms the basis of an exciting way of viewing man and his problems; it follows the newest European approaches to psychotherapy; it grows out of phenomenology. It is *Daseinanalyse,* the approach to behavior stemming from existentialist thought.

Footnotes

¹ C. Gilbert Wrenn, "Philosophical and Psychological Bases of Personnel Services in Education," *Fifty-Eighth Yearbook, Part II, N.S.S.E.* (Chicago: University of Chicago Press, 1959), Chap. 3, p. 41.

² Carl Rogers, *Counseling and Psychotherapy* (Boston: Houghton Mifflin Company, 1942), pp. 78-79. (This reference is relatively old, but Rogers' more recent writings have not departed from the stated beliefs.)

³ Carl Rogers, *Client-Centered Therapy.* Boston: Houghton Mifflin Co., 1951, pp. 483-522 *passim.*

⁴ Donald Snygg and A. W. Combs, *Individual Behavior* (New York: Harper & Row, Publishers, 1949).

⁵ A favorite illustration of meaning criterion used by Herbert Feigl in his epistemology classes at the University of Minnesota, quoted from V. C. Aldrich, "Pictorial Meanings . . ." in H. Feigl and W. Sellars, *Readings in Philosophical Analysis* (New York: Appleton-Century-Crofts, Inc., 1949), p. 176 f.

⁶ Snygg and Combs, *op. cit.,* 310.

⁷ Snygg and Combs, *op. cit.,* 13-33.

⁸ This need not be the case, if one grants a "supernatural force" as one more influence in the phenomenal field, or if one grants a supernatural Creator of the total scheme of existence, as some of the religious existentialists have done. This, however, is the "leap of faith" which admits of no empirical documentation or proof. The system of phenomenology can be explained parsimoniously without it; with it, the relationships between what is "in" the phenomenal field becomes tenuous, requiring more concessions than most phenomenologists are willing to grant.

⁹ Snygg and Combs, *op. cit.,* p. 41.

¹⁰ Snygg and Combs, *op. cit.,* p. 43.

¹¹ Snygg and Combs, *op. cit.,* p. 43.

¹² James Cribbin, "A Critique of the Philosophy of Modern Guidance." A summary of his dissertation. Reported in Gail Farwell and Herman Peters, *Guidance Readings for Counselors* (Chicago: Rand McNally Company, 1960), pp. 82-83.

¹³ Cribbin, *op. cit.,* 91-93.

¹⁴ Carl Rogers, *Client-Centered Therapy,* p. 532.

¹⁵ Mathewson, *op. cit.,* 198.

¹⁶ *Ibid.,* 199.

¹⁷ *Ibid.,* 140.

¹⁸ *Ibid.,* 142.

¹⁹ *Ibid.,* 147.

²⁰ *Ibid.,* 155.

²¹ C. Gilbert Wrenn, *op. cit.* See especially pages 74-80.

²² Wrenn, *op. cit.,* p. 76. All the quotations which follow have been from the same article.

CHAPTER FOUR

❖ Propositions and a Framework for the Philosophy of Guidance for the Future

Introduction

Wrenn's previously quoted statement is worthy of repetition:

> . . . highly fallible set of convictions . . . spread out for public view. They are bare and unprotected, fair targets. . . .

The outline of this chapter is simple. First, the basic questions that have plagued guidance philosophy will be identified. Second, there will be a listing of the basic demands the literature has indicated should be met by a philosophy of guidance. Third, propositions derived from the literature will be noted. Fourth, the presuppositions underlying the propositions will be compared with those of the *Daseinanalyse* model. The resultant comparison will have implications for some important aspects of guidance in the future.

It may be because the presuppositions underlying the many statements of credo in guidance have been clouded by semantic confusions and unexamined assumptions that guidance has found itself without a consistent philosophical position.

Basic Questions to Be Discussed

It is upon the resolution of certain key questions that any philosophy depends.

a. *What is the nature of reality?*
Is there some "Grand Plan" being worked out in the universe, or is everything in it the result of accidental or purely physical happenings? Is there some other possibility as yet unexplored?

b. *What is man's place in the universe?*
Does man have "duties," or are all "oughts" meaningless terms? What are man's limitations? What of his relationships to others? To himself? What is the nature of "need"?

c. *What is knowledge?*
Whence comes knowledge? What are the "proofs" of the things we "know"? Does the possession of knowledge entail any "duties"? Does the possession of skills contain or imply any "oughts"?

d. *How free is man?*
Is freedom an ontological fact, or an illusion? Does "natural law" prescribe or describe our world? Are all happenings dependent upon all others? Is everything that happens—all phenomena—purposive and planned? Is a supernatural world a possibility? A probability? Shall we act on the possibility of such a realm?

e. *What things (events, people) are of most worth?*
Or is it even possible to assign relative worth to these? Are there some items of our existence—or preceding it—which cannot appear on such a scale? Are there "absolutes"?

f. *Are there mandatory goals for society? For individuals?*
What is the nature of any such mandates? Are the goals of any given group just as "good" as those of any other? Given certain goals, what are the relative worths of various means toward these goals? Is "responsibility" a meaningless term? Does it have only consensus as its validation? Is this all that is needed?

These are basic questions in general philosophy. They are also questions important to every thoughtful counselor and to others who are involved in guidance. The same questions, in various altered forms, arise again and again in psychological interviews.

Perhaps more directly addressed to the daily frame of reference of guidance are subsidiary questions such as these:

1. By what criteria shall decisions be made?
2. How is accurate prediction possible?

3. Who shall counsel? By what authority? In what conditions? By what method? For what end?
4. What are the "needs" of human beings? Of a *given client?*
5. Does any known philosophy hold hope for systematizing the findings of recent research in guidance and therapy?
6. How can counselors best be trained?
7. How can guidance work be made more effective in relieving human suffering?

All positions in general philosophy have attempted to answer the previously listed questions, and via inference (or extrapolation) can be said to have attempted answers to the philosophical queries of the counselors. However, it is the contention of this study that *only one* position in general philosophy has been addressed primarily to the counselors' questions. It grew out of thoughtful analysis of living and brought about a method of therapy. It is the philosophy of *Daseinanalyse.*

Daseinanalyse is a way of viewing the human condition which is immediately recognizable to every counselor on the level of feeling, if not on the level of cognition of terms.

The literature of guidance has revealed what is demanded of any philosophy of guidance. Henry Borow demanded that any framework for guidance must take into account dispositional aspects of human behavior, and not try to reduce to operational language that which by its very nature, its unique quality, does not admit of quantitative, operational casting.

. . . Since . . . the strategy of much current research in counseling and psychotherapy is rooted in operationism, a few dissenting comments are in order . . . it is dispositional terms (e.g., compliant, manic, anxious) for which operational definitions are commonly contrived . . . dispositional terms are logically distinct from operational terms. Unlike the latter, they carry implications of an indeterminate kind and number and cannot be defined by single, specific acts or discrete behavioral items. [This passage is a composite of Borow's correspondence with Vernon Dolphin, a former colleague of his.]

To the foregoing discussion Borow adds:

. . . neither can clearly theoretical terms be operationally defined. Such constructs as the unconscious, guilt and overcompensation, like the term electromagnetic action in physical science, are essentially non-instantial variables. They do not exist in the data language, even though we may come to some agreement about their indicators in the world of observation. Operational terms tend to be descriptive in character; theoretical terms are explanatory.[1]

From this basic position, Borow sets up what he calls "fruitful direction for future research." It is this phase of his work which is most important for determining the basic demands which a philosophy of guidance for the future must meet.

Any adequate philosophy of guidance, and any "fruitful research" in guidance *must provide*:

1. *Order and standardization to the descriptive language in the field.* Borow cited the work of Shoben, Rotter, and his own examination of the literature which turned up a host of labels and terminological confusions on such basic items as "adjustment," "mental health," "psychological normality," and others.

2. *More evidence on precisely what occurs in the counseling process.* Borow hinted at the belief that counseling may turn out to be a function of a particular counselor, a particular client, and the particular problem. If this is the case, it will have important implications for the philosophy of guidance.

It is interesting in this discussion that Borow quoted Pepinsky's statement on the situation. Pepinsky's statement implied a specific directiveness for the "good of the client." His statement is perfectly phenomenological and consistent. It will also be shown to be ethically justifiable under *Daseinanalyse* philosophy. This is only one example of the more comprehensive character of *Daseinanalyse* thinking over that of strict phenomenological or realist thinking. His quotation:[2]

> The counselor must specify the kinds of responses he wants the client to make as an end-product of counseling and (he must specify) the decisions by which he makes it maximally likely that such client responses will occur.

Borow's third criterion was that research must provide information on analytic research that will feed back to theory and nourish it.

Here Borow pointed out a significant fact about past research in counseling. This fact is of vital importance and deserves much more publicity than it has received.

Borow stressed that the research dealing with counseling *process* has been directed to counselors in the mass. He contended that more basic to the effectiveness of guidance would be research directed toward a given counselor in a special type of problem situation with a given type of client, i.e., the personalistic view which Allport has recommended for so long. Borow did not merely state that this was desirable, but that this was vital. Counseling to him was viewed as interaction of two persons, not that of a system and a person. Such research would be tedious, he admitted, but records of what was intended and what transpired in the process was deemed essential.

To Borow's listing of what an adequate future pattern in guidance thinking must be, others added their *sine qua nons* and their desired changes.

Tyler recommended that guidance follow a course of action which, if pursued, would lead in the direction of *Daseinanalyse* philosophy and psychology. She challenged the theory that the best therapy is that which produces the most change—challenged it by proposing a new type of therapy and counseling, predicated on *minimum* change. This was in keeping with her statements as to man's dignity, integrity, and uniqueness.

> Therapy generally has as its goal personality change; counseling attempts to bring about the best possible utilization of what the person already has. . . .
> Is it really true that the therapy that produces the most changes is the best therapy? Would it not be possible to make the opposite assumption and deliberately set as our goal "Minimal change therapy"? This would be a kind of undertaking that would fit well with the rest of the activities that go on under the name counseling. We would try in each case to help the person discover some unlocked path in which he could move forward, develop his own unique personality, and thus transcend rather than delve into the anxieties and conflicts in which he is now enmeshed. . . .
> One way of characterizing this kind of therapeutic counseling is to say that its basic premises come from the psychology of development and individual differences rather than the psychology of adjustment. Its most fundamental assumption is that there are many different ways of living an individual life richly and well, and that it is natural for a person to continue to develop throughout his life in his own unique way. We work with nature instead of fighting or ignoring it.[3]

Her thesis was clear. It accentuated strengths rather than concentrating on *trying* to clear up weaknesses. It stressed letting the person be what he is rather than molding him into what he is not.

Harrison spoke in a similar vein.

. . . discover the potential of each child and see that each one has his fair *opportunity* to develop that potential to the utmost for the highest good that he is able to offer, both to himself and to the world.

One of the fundamental beliefs undergirding the guidance and personnel movement has been respect for the individual. But caught up in a contagious frenzy for survival, it is easy to relegate concern for specific individuals to a secondary position. We can also forget that physical survival is not always worth the struggle, or that physical survival is hardly worth the indignities to man.[4]

Both these writers were speaking on behalf of a philosophy of guidance which calls for deep commitment to personal meanings on the part of the client, and for a commitment on the part of the counselor to do everything within his power to free the client to follow these commitments. This demand added impetus to those of Borow and Pepinsky previously noted.

Perhaps most difficult of the demands which a unified philosophy of guidance must face would be that of reconciling the views of those who have based their systems of values on "eternal verities" and religious principles with those who have insisted that no supernatural source exists, or that, if it does, it does not lend itself to verification, and that counseling can proceed without reference to it. This quandary seemed to cause Wrenn to doubt his tentative conclusion that the instrumentalist position was the one which was most congruent with guidance. *Daseinanalyse* philosophy has encompassed both forms of thinking, just as did its parent philosophy of existentialism. There is room for a Sartre and also for a Kierkegaard.

This is not just the mark of an eclectic philosophy. It is a genuine assimilation of two modes of thinking into a framework which can become a vital force in guidance. It might well be disseminated and discussed in guidance training programs.

The Semantic Confusion of "Meeting Needs"

Another demand which recurred in the literature was that guidance must meet the needs of the student. To date there has been no clarification of this concept in the literature of guidance. This lack has resulted in much confusion.

There is no argument that guidance should help meet "the needs" of students if it is to exist at all. The straw man who takes the brunt of those demanding that the student's needs be met is only a straw man.

B. Paul Komisar, in an unpublished paper entitled "The Pedagogical Concept for Need," presented a clear analysis of the concept which can be applied with little difficulty to guidance.

Stripping away the semantic confusions, Komisar arrived at two, or perhaps three, categories of need, used in two very clearly spelled out ways.

A. THE PRESCRIPTIVE USES OF "NEED"

1. To make rules   (Students need 15 credits for graduation.)
2. To make specific directives   (This boy needs homework.)
3. To report requirements   (If you want to improve you need to practice.)

B. THE MOTIVATION USES OF "NEED"

1. To report motives   (He needs—wants—the book.)
2. To report motivation dispositions   (He needs—periodically wants —recognition.)

The third category which Komisar admitted as a very doubtful possibility for legitimate use is "Deficit States." In its present state, however, it was a moot point, Komisar felt, whether such usage was significant, trivial, or redundant.[5]

If, taking the foregoing theorists as fairly representative of the field of guidance, a composite list of the demands to be made upon any philosophy of guidance were formulated, they might be stated tentatively as:

1. Freeing the individual to pursue his own life-style
2. Not endangering society (but this must be qualified)
3. Recognizing an objective order "out there" which operates in a predictable manner
4. Positing a "phenomenal field" which contains the limits of man's knowledge of self
5. Recognizing the existence of certain values which permeate the lives of most men, past and present
6. Viewing man as an emergent, not static, being
7. Viewing inference from past experience as the chief source of knowledge

8. Realizing that some values are generically shared, that others are personal and unique

9. Accommodating both natural and supernatural possibilities

10. Positing a choice-laden universe, with the nature of choice explained

11. Reconciling responsibility of the individual with the "deterministic," finite qualities of human existence

12. Viewing cause and effect reasoning as valid, and prediction as possible within limits

13. Meeting life needs of students, in the sense of making their lives vital and meaningful

14. Explaining and clarifying semantic confusions, especially in defining the goals and limits of guidance

15. Examining the counseling process as it relates to a given, individual situation

16. Clarifying the legitimacy of counselor direction in the counseling situation

17. Giving meaning to life in a complex, confusing society

The above charges to a philosophy of guidance are great. *Daseinanalyse* thinking has been proposed to serve this function. What it is and how it serves these functions must be spelled out.

Daseinanalyse theory grew out of existential philosophy. The former must be examined in the light of the latter. It will be necessary to explore both concurrently in the following pages.

Existential Psychology: Extension of Phenomenology

As we have shown in Chapter Three, the basic position of realism in guidance has slowly merged into a form of thought called phenomenology. The basic reason for the merging was that the framework of realism did not provide enough "room" for the psychologist or the counselor. It was not enough that a rather stable order of things existed; the guidance worker and the psychologist were constantly confronted with beings who could not perceive the presupposed "objective" order of things. The frustration of trying to "interpret" reality to beings in trouble, trying to arrive at a level of communication other than intellectual, has been written in the history of the more directive forms of psychoanalysis and counseling. The psychological counselor came to accept the fact that the underlying "reality" of the physical world and the "generally accepted" meanings of Western culture were often not at all those of a given client. The logical step, though long in arriving, was the move toward a phenomenological frame of reference. The client's meanings, his feelings about reality, his hopes and sorrows were finally recognized as of prime importance and as indeed the only reality he could perceive, given his own "field" and self-concept.

Even in accepting phenomenology as a psychological basis for dealing with human behavior, counselors and psychologists created difficulties of the same stripe as those created by psychologists when psychology was trying to become "accepted" as a science. They strived for an almost mathematical precision, a closed system, a fully explained pattern and theory of behavior. This brought about the difficulty of dealing with choice-behavior in satisfactory terms. As one scholar has stated, "It is the mark of a mature mind to be able to live with an incomplete world view." Phenomenology tried to move toward too "pat" a system, perhaps, too deterministic an explanation of complex human behavior.

One of the cardinal principles of phenomenology has been that introspection alters the field and is therefore an illegitimate source of knowledge, or at least an unreliable explanatory technique. Phenomenologists, in examining their own theoretical foundations, have not heeded their own advice. They have used a reflective introspection of what takes place in human behavior to arrive at this conclusion. By declaring introspection nonvalid, they have been consistent, but have lost something in the process.

In Chapter Three, we showed that phenomenology was based upon a strictly deterministic, naturalistic view of human behavior. The basic postulates of phenomenology as stated by one of its leading proponents were as follows:

1. All behavior is lawful. This is a necessary assumption of any sytem, since change behavior would be unpredictable.
2. Behavior is completely determined by and pertinent to the phenomenological field of the behaving organism. By phenomenological field is meant the universe, including himself, as experienced by the behaver at the moment.
3. There is some relationship between the phenomenological fields of different individuals. This is a necessary assumption, since control is impossible if one individual is unable to affect another's field. The locus of the relationship, usually presumed to be an *underlying* reality, is not open to observation.

4. Greater precision of behavior (learning) is concomitant with greater differentiation of the phenomenological field. Another characteristic . . . is that (phenomenological fields) are fluid and shifting; their phenomena are continually reshaped and given new meanings by the character of the total configuration. Memories . . . are strongly affected in this way.

5. The characteristics of the parts of the phenomenological field are determined by the character of the field itself. More specifically, the direction and degree of differentiation are determined by the phenomenological needs of the behaver. . . . The fundamental need in a phenomenological system appears to be the preservation of the organization and integrity of the phenomenological self and especially that part of the field which is the phenomenal self, whence our tendency to remain unaware of, or to reject with emotion, data inconsistent with our own beliefs.

6. Differentiation takes time. It follows from this principle that the way to accelerate learning is to arrange the situation so that the required differentiations are either more obvious or are unnecessary.[6]

In the same article the author listed the *advantages* of the phenomenological system. Chief among these he stated were:

1. A phenomenological system is anthropomorphic. Its data are stated in terms of immediate experience and require no translation to make them meaningful.

2. It is concerned with the prediction and control of individual behavior, a field closed to objective systems because of their necessary assumption of variability in individual behavior. For this reason, psychiatrists, applied psychologists, and teachers when dealing with individuals commonly adopt a phenomenological view. This accounts for the great use by these groups of psychoanalysis, Gestalt, and private non-academic systems which have large phenomenological components. The use of a general field can result in the prediction of general, normative behavior only.

3. As compared with the objective approach, the phenomenological approach is more inclusive. Individual behavior cannot be predicted from normative behavior. On the other hand, accuracy in predicting individual behavior makes possible the prediction of normative behavior as well.

4. . . . The predictive advantage of postulating only one process, which is descriptive rather than causal or explanatory.[7]

From the postulates and the alleged advantages of phenomenology in dealing with human behavior, and from the features noted in Chapter Three, it is deemed advisable to view existential psychotherapy and *Daseinanalyse* philosophy as an extension of phenomenology. Phenomenology served well the purpose of making the counselor and the therapist aware of the importance of the client's feelings and his *views* of "reality." But the strictly deterministic orientation of phenomenology has been called to question.

What does he mean by 'deterministic'!?

The Daseinanalyse Point of View and Related Views

The various current emphases in European psychotherapy and psychoanalysis are, by the statements of their practitioners, extensions of phenomenology. The reason for the existence of these thought currents is that phenomenology again did not provide a framework wide enough and vital enough to meet the requirements of psychology and therapy. From this lack of ability to encompass man's *felt problems* emerged *Daseinanalyse* and concomitant forms of existential psychology and philosophical thinking.

Several terms must be examined at the outset. Existential analysis (*Daseinanalyse*), existential psychotherapy, and existential philosophy are closely related, yet each must be understood separately.

Existential philosophy is an exciting thought current within general philosophy. It has taken several forms: some, atheistic; others, religious. Usually existentialist philosophers deride the "pat" systems of the older, more established philosophical creeds. The existentialists take as their point of emphasis the mode of reality most meaningful to man: his own existence. Among the leading proponents of existentialism vital to the concepts discussed herein are Jean-Paul Sartre, Gabriel Marcel, Paul Tillich, Merleau-Ponty, Heidegger, Berdyaev, and others.

Existential psychotherapy is the application of some vital, key ideas from the thinking of existentialist philosophers to the science of treating mental and emotional disorders. Some would not yet label existential psychotherapy as a school of thought, but the writings of those employing such an approach indicate several methods and concepts which constitute more than a chance congruence of eclectics. Procedures vary surprisingly little among religious and non-religious practitioners employing existentialist concepts in therapy.

Daseinanalyse, sometimes called existential analysis, involves more than empathy. It is a system calling for a reconstruction of and a "living along with" the client which exceeds the bounds of merely trying to understand one's client. It employs many insights from psychoanalysis, phenomenology, and existential philosophy. It calls for a re-examination of the question usually in the mind of a therapist: under what conditions would I behave or feel like that? The question in the mind of the *Daseinanalyse* practitioner is how can I *experience with him* (the client) what he is going through, so that I may better understand his meanings, values, and choices? Existential anxiety is viewed as a vital factor in determining life-style and choices.

These distinctions are important, since the literature coming from the continent is confusing unless the terminology is kept in mind.

In the field of guidance and in cases of minor therapy involving choice-anxiety *Daseinanalyse* appears to be of prime importance. It combines the "realism orientation" upon which guidance is based with a more vital brand of phenomenology. The term "existential phenomenology" entered the literature in 1960. This term may or may not be more acceptable in this country than the word *Dasein-analyse*, since "analysis" is a cognate which may be unacceptable to nondirective counselors. The term *Daseinanalyse* has appeared only twice in guidance journals, both times in connection with nondirective counseling. Dreyfus[8] identified the working assumptions of Rogerian counseling with those of existentialism and made reference to May's book which described *Daseinanalyse*. Rogers[9] favorably reviewed the same book, but termed the case studies employing the approach "disappointing."

Since the introduction of the term into the guidance literature was so recent, it is not possible to ascertain the measure of acceptance it will receive by leading writers. However, the presuppositional framework which appears to underlie *Daseinanalyse* also appears to provide (a) satisfactory answers or approaches to the questions at the beginning of this chapter; (b) working hypotheses which may satisfy the technique-minded practitioner; (c) the satisfaction of the demands for "vital, individual" guidance and counseling; and (d) a network of presuppositions which is acceptable to those who have done most of the philosophical writing in the guidance literature. It is to the explication of these points that the following remarks are addressed.

In summary it might be said that *Daseinanalyse* or, as it will be termed interchangeably hereafter in this study, "existential phenomenology," follows the presuppositions of phenomenology mentioned previously with these important exceptions:

1. *Daseinanalyse* emphasizes the fact that, because of existential anxiety, one may live in two or more mutually exclusive worlds; phenomenology emphasizes the centrality or unity of the experiences of the organism. The *Daseinanalyse* theorist feels that the latter statement may be true of lower forms of life, but that man partakes of a different mode of existence (Vorhandensein) and therefore faces meanings which often complicate his life meanings.

2. *Daseinanalyse* attempts to reconstruct the meaning-structure of the world of the individual, or the conflicting structures of his two or more worlds of meanings and influences; it explores how and why meanings have changed. Phenomenology stresses the present field of influences.

3. Phenomenology stresses awarenesses, consciousness, perceptions. *Daseinanalyse* is concerned with the total meaning-structure of the client: his life style, his views of life and death, his word choices, and all aspects of his relating to life.

To these differences should be appended a fourth vital difference. There is an inherent belief that certain key concepts influence behavior although they do not admit of measurement. They are of the deepest fabric of human existence, and can be marked "existent" only by the examination of deep human feelings as they are experienced by everyone, and as they have been recorded by great authors. Those interested in these existentialist concepts might find interesting Heidegger's *Vorhandensein-Dasein* dichotomy; Binswanger's *Umwelt, Mitwelt,* and *Eigenwelt;* Tillich's *kairos,* and others from current *Daseinanalyse* writings. According to the existential phenomenologists, to explain these in behavioristic terms would be tenuous and reductionistic.

Perhaps the most meaningful way to approach the topic of what existential phenomenology means for guidance and therapy is to present first the introductory description of *Daseinanalyse* by May. He cited as the founders of present-day *Daseinanalyse* practice such men as Ludwig Binswanger, A. Storch, M. Boss, G. Bally, Roland Kuhn in Switzerland; J. H. Van Den Berg and F. J. Buytendijk in Holland; Eugene Minkowski, Erwin Strauss (now in the United States), and V. E. von Gebsattel in Germany. He typed the Germans as phenomenologists who laid the groundwork for what has developed into existential phenomenology. May traced the philosophical foundations of the movement to an attempt to be more, not less, empirical. The newer thinking is an attempt to see the individual man as a meaningful whole, not as the product of our preconceptions, as a system-fitting mosaic piece, or as a statistical probability. May's *Existence* is "must" reading for counselors.

May sums up the contribution of existential therapy as follows:

> The fundamental contribution of existential therapy is its understanding of man as *being*. It does not deny the validity of dynamisms and the study of specific behavior patterns in their rightful places. But it holds that drives or dynamisms, by whatever name one calls them, can be understood only in the context of the *structure of the existence* of the person we are dealing with. The distinctive character of existential analysis is, thus, that it is concerned with *ontology*, the science of being, and with *Dasein*, the existence of this particular being sitting opposite the psychotherapist.[10]

On the nature of the interview, May says:

> The grasping of the being of the other person occurs on a quite different level from our knowledge of specific things about him.[11]

May differentiates quite clearly between "knowing" and "knowing about" a person. Throughout the book he returns to the use of the existentialist term for the existentialist-psychological interview, the "encounter." It is the mutual interaction of the beings. The help relationship implies much more than the analysis of the one by the other. This will be discussed.

On the implications for therapy, May states that technique follows understanding. This is exactly the reverse of the usual Western approach in psychology.

On the matter of techniques used, May states that many techniques are used, but that they are chosen in full knowledge of what their use *presupposes*, not just as another form of eclecticism. This latter statement, and perhaps also most of the statements in May's book, are a direct refutation of an undocumented statement in a widely read reference book in psychology. The quotation:

> Phenomenology, the science of phenomena, is a *presuppositionless*, but systematic, exploration and description of experience, including both acts, and contents. . . .[12]

In both phenomenology and existential phenomenology, presuppositions *can* be identified, and are vital to the application of these systems to the study of human behavior. There was no documentation for the statement that phenomenology is presuppositionless. However, at least the commonly used brand of phenomenology, that of Snygg and Combs, does have presuppositions which are important to the system (see Chapter Three).

May stated that certain questions determine the technique to be used in existential therapy. They are, "What will best reveal the existence of this particular patient at this moment in his history?" and, "What will best illuminate his being-in-the-world?" [13]

May mentioned that Carl Rogers has written in what amounts to an existentialist tone. The quotation is precisely that, and is worth repetition. It is almost exactly the credo which a Sartrean-like therapist might utter.

> I launch myself into the therapeutic relationship having a hypothesis, or a faith, that my liking, my confidence, and my understanding of the other person's inner world, will lead to a significant process of becoming. I enter the relationship not as a scientist, not as a physician who can accurately diagnose and cure, but as a person, entering into a personal relationship. Insofar as I see him only as an object, the client will tend to become only an object.
>
> I risk myself, because if, as the relationship deepens, what develops is a failure, a regression, a repudiation of me and the relationship by the client, then I sense that I will lose myself, or a part of myself. At times this risk is very real, and is very keenly experienced.
>
> I let myself go into the immediacy of the relationship where it is my total organism which takes over and is sensitive to the relationship, not simply my consciousness. I am not consciously responding in a planful or analytic way, but simply in an unreflective way to the other individual, my reaction being based (but not consciously) on my total organismic sensitivity to this other person. I live the relationship on this basis.[14]

Titus' definition of existentialism seems to parallel Rogers' feelings.

> Existentialism is an emphasis on the uniqueness and primacy of existence in the sense of the inner, immediate experience of self-awareness. The fundamental drive or urge is to exist and to be recognized as an individual person. The most meaningful point of reference for any person is his own immediate consciousness, which cannot be contained in systems or abstractions.[15]

Existence connotes responsible, vital, meaningful, emerging life. It is not merely "living" which is a generic term for all forms of life. Here a sharp distinction is drawn between two modes of life.

existence precedes essence
                               Sartre

They are termed *Vorhandensein* and *Dasein* by Heidegger in his *Sein und Zeit*. The former refers to things (trees, animals, and sometimes to objects), the latter is a mode of life which is found only in man. It is a life aware of itself and aware of its ultimate nonbeing. Even in this dichotomy there is a great difference in the way an individual man partakes of this *Dasein*.

The Mature Person

As shown in Chapter Three, the mature person has been described in the guidance literature as outgoing, responsible, civic-minded. Maturity, or full partaking of man's mode of existence (*Dasein*), has been described quite differently by the existentialist philosopher and the existentialist psychologist. There are two basic types of existentialist, the religious and the nonreligious. Jean-Paul Sartre represents the latter.

Sartre begins with the presupposition that man is on his own in a universe which does not need him, and is hostile to him. He denies the existence of a god, eternal or fixed values, and a fixed human nature. He has no patience with evolutionary philosophies of history, especially Marxism, because they deny the fact that man is fully responsible for his choices. Man is free, and this leads to grave responsibility. Man can become what he wills and works for. The mature man is the man who is courageous enough to realize that man is what he makes himself. Sartre demands choice-making and action. If man is unhappy, it is because he has not made vital choices. A style of living without commitment is devoid of real existence, and leads to despair. A style of living which moves toward what man desires to become can be thrilling, worth the trouble of living.[16]

Sartre calls existentialism the "most austere of philosophies." He denies that the term should be applied to many groups of people who delight in daringly wearing it as a label. He states that "it is intended strictly for specialists and philosophers." There are Christian existentialists and atheistic existentialists (among the former Karl Jaspers, N. Berdyaev, Gabriel Marcel, P. Tillich, and others; among the latter Heidegger, Sartre, and other French existentialists). Sartre identifies the chief common trait in both types: existence precedes essence.[17] This is the fundamental presupposition of both schools.

To the atheistic existentialist there is no god, and therefore there is no mind (or Mind) to conceive of "man's nature," no "designer" and hence no design.

Man, first of all, exists, turns up, appears on the scene, and, only afterwards, defines himself. If man, as the existentialist conceives him, is indefinable, it is because at first he is nothing. Only afterward will he be something, and he himself will have made what he will be. . . . Not only is man what he conceives himself to be, but he is only what he wills himself to be after his thrust toward existence. . . . Man is nothing else but what he makes of himself. Such is the first principle of existentialism. It is also what is called subjectivity, the name we are labeled with when charges are brought against us. But what do we mean by this, if not that man has a greater dignity than a stone or table? . . . man first exists . . . hurls himself toward a future . . . conscious of imagining himself . . . in the future . . . man will be what he will have planned to be. Not what he will want to be.[18]

Sartre states that existentialism's first move is to make every man aware of what he is and to make the full responsibility of his existence rest on him. He further stresses the concept that when man chooses a value or life-style, he is not only choosing for himself but for all mankind. If one chooses monogamy, Christianity, or any other vital commitment, it must be because of personal, deep feelings that this is the life-style best for man. One must do his utmost to further the chosen course of action for all men.[19]

At this point it might be well to try to state this position in phenomenological terms. As shown in Chapter Three, Snygg and Combs make much of the concept of "proprium" or "that which one conceives of as part of himself." This is normally limited to one's body, plus, perhaps, one's clothing. Sometimes it extends to one's loved ones, and to one's dearly held ideas. If a phenomenologist (such as most nondirective counselors have maintained that they are) finds difficulty in accepting the "One chooses for all mankind" idea from Sartre, it might be advisable to think of *mankind generically —a part of oneself, of one's proprium.* This is little different from the concept of Christian brotherly love, the Golden Rule, or Kant's Categorical Imperative, but it calls for commitment in every action because man is alone in the universe with his fellows. They share his predicament. They feel joy, sorrow, sickness, loneliness much as he does. Man's only source of earthly consolation is his fellow man. To accept Sartre's call to action in choice-making and commitment is an ennobling act.

Sartre answers the charges of many that existentialism leads to anguish, loneliness. He relates this to the principle above: choosing in all one's actions and commitments for all mankind. When one makes choices which involve heavy responsibility for the lives of others, such as the orders of a general in battle, one feels anguish.

> All leaders know this anguish. That doesn't keep them from acting; on the contrary, it is the very condition of their action. For it implies that they envisage a number of possibilities, and when they choose one, they realize that it has value only because it is chosen.[20]

Decision without action is for Sartre no decision at all.

In the matter of the nonexistence of God, the atheistic existentialist does not glory in it; he is distressed in the extreme. Life would be so simple if only God (and eternal values, the good life prescribed, etc.) did exist.

> . . . all possibility of *finding* values in a heaven of ideas disappears along with Him; . . . the fact is we are on a plane where there are only men. Dostoievsky said, "If God didn't exist, everything would be possible." That is the very starting point of existentialism. Indeed, everything is possible if God does not exist, and as a result man is forlorn, because neither within him nor without does he find anything to cling to. He can't start making excuses for himself.
>
> If existence really does precede essence, there is no explaining things away by reference to a fixed and given human nature. In other words, there is no determinism, man is free, man is freedom. On the other hand, if God does not exist, we find no values or commands to turn to which legitimize our conduct. So, in the bright realm of values, we have no excuse behind us, nor justification before us. We are alone, with no excuses.[21]

It is significant that Sartre uses the plural form "WE" in his work. This stresses his constant belief that man and his fellows must shape their existence in mutual respect and cooperation. Sincere commitment is the whole basis of man's hope in a life of anguish and loneliness.

> . . . man is condemned to be free. Condemned, because he did not create himself, yet in other respects is free; because, once thrown into the world, he is responsible for everything he does.[22]

This is different from the simple phenomenological edict that all acts are determined by the phenomenal field, that choice is a sham.

The task ahead is to reconcile or analyze how the phenomenologist can move in the direction of the vital quality of Sartre's proposal, and if to do so is desirable.

Sartre also made a point which has not been stated in the literature of counseling to date. He remarked that, when one is faced with choice-anxiety in a decision-making situation, the fact that he chooses or does not choose to go to an "adviser" of some sort is in itself a decision, and therefore he is in part responsible for the final choice made even if he follows the advice of another. Also, the person he chooses to see about it (priest, psychologist, a given friend, or other) is an indication of what course of action he tends toward, prior to the interview.

> . . . You already knew, more or less, just about what advice he was going to give you. In other words, choosing your adviser is involving yourself.[23]

All systems of counseling insist that the ultimate responsibility for choice rests with the counselee. Sartre has justified this position further, by including the *type* of person *chosen* as an indicator of one's involvement in the outcome. If one is dissatisfied with the "trend" in a counseling situation, he is free to discontinue (according to all schools of thought in counseling). Indeed, many do discontinue. Could this be because they have not found the trend or the advice they half-consciously demanded from the situation, and have moved to another "counseling" situation (friend, wife, husband, other psychologist) where what they hear will lead to the course of action they feel they ought to take? The nondirective theory of counseling anticipates this and defines the situation as one in which the counselor is reflecting and clarifying the opinions and feelings of the client. The term "supportive therapy" has been used to denote affirmation of the choice (in more directive counseling atmospheres) made by the client when he appears consonant with "reality" in his choice of action. Sartre implements his point that there is no escape from the individual's own responsibility for choices. He has, perhaps, given even better arguments for this position than has the guidance literature. No counselor appeared to have questioned this stand in the matter.

Through all of his novels and his philosophical writings, Sartre stresses that a man's acts define the man. He is not a creature made to react as a coward, a hero, or a delinquent by a deterministic universe, but rather he has chosen his role by his acts or by choosing inaction ("choosing not to choose—itself a choice"). Existentialism, thus, is not a pessimism; man's destiny is within himself; he can be what he takes action to become. Involvement, commitment, action, responsibility, feeling for one's fellows—this is the crux of existentialist philosophy.

The counselor who sincerely shares the basic outlook of Sartre on life's meaning will approach the counseling situation with a renewed seriousness. The full implications will be spelled out after a discussion of religious existentialists and their views. To the serious-minded counselor or counselor-educator, many of the implications are obvious.

Man must be subject, not object. This theory is the only one which gives man dignity and worth. Each man must be treated as an experiencing being worthy of being treated as one himself desires to be treated, for he is part of the proprium of his brother.

Sartre hints at the *Daseinanalyse* approach when he speaks of the "human condition."

> If it is impossible to find in every man some universal essence which would be human nature, yet there does exist a universal human condition. It's not by chance that today's thinkers speak more readily of man's condition than of his nature. By condition they mean, more or less definitely, the *a priori* limits which outline man's fundamental situation in the universe. Historical situations vary. A man may be born a slave . . . what does not vary is the necessity for him to exist in the world, to be at work there, to be there in the midst of other people, and to be mortal there. Though the configurations may differ, at least none of them are completely strange to me. . . . Every configuration can be understood, even the Chinese, the Indian, or the Negro. . . . There is always a way to understand the idiot, the child, the savage, the foreigner, provided one has the necessary information.[24]

It is precisely this "feeling with" and understanding the life-style and meanings of the client that *Daseinanalyse* strives to accomplish.

Sartre's closest approach to the subject of counseling arose in a questioning-and-debate session with Marxists. The matter under discussion was the case of a young man who came to Sartre for counsel.

> . . . I shall cite the case of one of my students who came to see me under the following circumstances: his father was on bad terms with his mother, and, moreover, was inclined to be a collaborationist; his

older brother had been killed in the German offensive of 1940, and the young man, with somewhat immature but generous feelings, wanted to avenge him. His mother lived alone with him, very much upset by the half-treason of her husband and the death of her older son; the boy was her only consolation.

The boy was faced with the choice of leaving for England and joining the Free French Forces—that is, leaving his mother behind— or remaining with his mother and helping her to carry on. He was fully aware that the woman lived only for him and that his going off—and perhaps his death—would plunge her into despair. He was also aware that every act he did for his mother's sake was a sure thing, in the sense that it was helping her to carry on, whereas every effort he made toward going off and fighting was an uncertain move which might run aground and prove completely useless. . . .[25]

In questioning Sartre about his advice to the young man (that he search his inner feelings, and that no one could choose for him), the Marxist stated,

He should have been answered. I would have tried to find out what he was capable of, his age, his financial possibilities, his relations with his mother. It's possible that I would have offered a probable opinion, but I would most certainly have tried to fix on a definite point of view, which, in practice, might have turned out to be a false one, but most certainly I would have had him do something.[26]

Sartre's answer to this:

If he comes to ask your advice, it's because he has already chosen his answer. I could very well have given him practical advice, but since it was freedom he was after, I wanted to let him decide. Besides, I knew what he was going to do, and that's what he did do.[27]

Note the similarities and differences here in Sartre's approach to counseling and that of Rogers. While Rogers and Sartre both avow the right and responsibility of the individual to make his own choices, Rogers feels that the role of the counselor is to clarify, reflect, open the alternatives to consideration. Sartre feels that the very choice of one counselor over another indicates that a choice has already been made. Sartre listens sympathetically, then casts the decision-making upon the client, which, ultimately, Rogers does. Sartre's action may be called "supportive" counseling in that he, as many of the clinical counseling schools might do, gives affirmation to the right, indeed to the responsibility, of the individual to follow through on what he has come to feel most deeply that he must do.

Sartre feels that to belabor the issue with "practical" advice or to becloud it with "alternatives" would be to infringe upon the commitments and deepest feelings, and upon the precious freedom of choice and action, of a human being who has within himself the power to decide and act in accordance with his own unique life-style.

By way of summary, Sartre represents existentialism of an atheistic or nonreligious sort. A system of counseling, if based upon his presuppositions, might resemble the following, a sort of "Sartre Resartus":

1. The dignity of each human being is presupposed, as is the freedom which comes from the lack of a priori "agenda" in man's world.

2. Each person is faced with real choices in a nondeterministic world. As man chooses, he chooses for all mankind.

3. Willing, without action to make vital the object of the willing, is an insignificant act. Actions taken define the life of man.

4. Counseling is a legitimate part of man's involvement with all others of his kind, but it must be of a very nondirective sort. To do otherwise would be to negate the fact that choice has already been made by the time one chooses a counselor. The choice of a given counselor implies the choice has been made.

5. If one accepts fully the need for action on the part of the counselor—his deepest commitments—one could argue that he must be *directive* when he feels that client is making a "wrong" (dangerous, immoral, dishonest) choice in order to maintain his own integrity as a person. However, it must be remembered that the whole act of counseling is voluntary because of the twin ideals of freedom and dignity assigned to the individual. The last thing an existentialist counselor would want to do is to give a person a chance to evade his own personal responsibility for choice and action, a chance to hide behind "authority" or the "collective demands of society." This would be a negation of what existentialism stands for. In that one structures the counseling situation toward a counselor's choice, to that degree does he infringe upon the freedom and commitment of the client. The counselor must weigh the degree of infringement against the alternative of saying, "Do what you know you must"; this is why the existentialist must call the counseling interview "the encounter," for there are two existential beings—each with commitments and life-styles. To the degree that they communicate at all, they become part of the ultimate decisions of the other.

6. Whatever techniques arise to the experienced counselor which seem pertinent "to this client in this situation" must be used. To do otherwise would be to sacrifice one's integrity and to do harm to one's client. This is different from "soft eclecticism" in that there must be

deeply felt reasons for doing what the counselor does, and these reasons must arise from the first three presuppositions listed here. Eclecticism without fundamental, deeply felt presuppositions is illegitimate to the existential counselor.

Religious Existentialism

Nonreligious existentialism as applied to counseling, using Sartre as a model, has been considered. Perhaps the thinking of the religious existentialist along these lines might be more in keeping with more of the counselors today. Counselors tend to come from the middle class, since most of them are recruited from the ranks of classroom teachers, who are in turn middle-class in the main. As such, the values of various religious systems, chiefly those of Christianity, hold the commitments and life-views of most of them. The basic premise of Sartre—that God does not exist and that man is left to his own devices—is perhaps more than most counselors can grant, yet many of Sartre's deeply felt statements strike a respondent chord in even the most religious men. The nature of religious existentialism and its application to counseling must be explored.

One who seeks more detailed accounts of religious existentialism than this study provides must go to the original sources of religious existentialist thought and by inference and extrapolation assemble it for themselves, for it has not been analyzed in the literature of guidance. The chief sources appear to be Karl Jaspers, Nicolai Berdyaev, Gabriel Marcel, Paul Tillich, Martin Buber, Jacques Maritain, and a few others whose works are footnoted by these men in their accounts of existentialism. The historical fountainhead of religious existentialism is Søren Kierkegaard. One who would seek to work out his personal religious-existential point of view must go to these sources for systematic treatment of the subject. The shades of existential meaning are different for each man, yet there is a common presuppositional framework which ties together what they deeply believe.

Søren Kierkegaard (1813-1855) is the usually acknowledged founder of religious existentialism. His personal life was pervaded by a sense of guilt, a bodily deformity, a strict upbringing in orthodox Lutheranism, and some severe personal disappointments. All these things colored his thinking. One of the best concise accounts of Kierkegaard's thought is perhaps that of Titus.

Titus stated that Kierkegaard wanted men to come to an understanding of their souls, their destiny, and the existence of an absolute God.

There are two great enemies of Christianity. One is Hegelian philosophy [and, presumably, all other "heavy" systems based on reason to the exclusion of personalism] so prevalent in his day. Abstract speculation, he believes, whether in the Cartesian or the Hegelian form, depersonalizes man and leaders to the impoverishment of life . . . this type of thinking tends to emphasize thought and to lose the thinker . . . scornful of all attempts to make Christianity reasonable or to come to its defense with intellectual arguments. He opposes those Protestants who interpret the Divine as immanent in the world of experience or God as expressing himself through nature, human history, and the lives of men. Philosophy and religion . . . deal with entirely different areas and do different things. Reason deals with time alone, whereas Christianity is concerned with eternity.

The second enemy is the conventional churchgoer, who imagines that he lives in a Christian community and thinks he is a Christian because he performs some "good works" and is a "good citizen." The unreflective or nominal church member may be a good functionary, but he has a depersonalized religion, and he may not know what it really means to *become* a Christian. Kierkegaard is highly critical of much in the Christianity or "Churchianity" of his day, especially the "unorthodox" Christians, with their evolutionary optimism, belief in human progress, confidence in reason, and faith in the goodness of man. He opposes the activism and the social Christianity which seem to imply that one can redeem men by making changes in the social order.[28]

Kierkegaard called for the same decision-translated-into-action which Sartre demands of the mature person. He affirmed the same responsibility of each individual for his own actions, yet he started from the premise of an all-powerful God. There is an unbridgeable gap between God and man. At this point man must abandon reason and embrace faith. In so doing he accepts many paradoxes, yet this for Kierkegaard is the only way. Man is finite, as is his reason. God is infinite. The dualism cannot be bridged by man by other than faith. God, of course, could at any time bridge the gap, but has given man the task of accepting on faith what his finite being cannot fathom. Man either is wholly obedient to God or wholly in rebellion; there is for Kierkegaard no middle ground.

Titus related Kierkegaard's "stages on life's road." These are found in other words but with essentially the same meaning in the writings of several theologians throughout history.

The first is the *aesthetic* stage, which is the life of the natural man who lives in sensuous enjoyment. This is the life of immediacy, in which the senses and emotions dominate the scene, and moral and religious demands are brushed aside. This stage by itself is the "path of perdition." The second is the *ethical* stage, where man arrives at the level of the universal human. Only on this level can man preserve aesthetic beauty and the rational and social order of things. At this point he begins to have some awareness of his vocation as a human being. At the third and highest stage, the religious man discovers the meaning of existence and sees himself as an individual who stands alone before God. Man's relation to God not only goes beyond the ethical stage but, at times, also may suspend it by doing that which appears to be "immoral." This is the teleological suspension of the ethical in response to what is believed to be the will of God.[29]

In Catholicism, Gabriel Marcel represents existentialist-type thinking, as does Jacques Maritain. The parallel current in Jewish thought is represented by Martin Buber. Again, the chief point of agreement among these theologians revolves about their presuppositions. All posit a God, which is uncomfortably (to the life-unexamined churchgoer) reminiscent of the deistic god: the designer who becomes an observer throughout man's life on earth; the spectator God who wants to see how man treats the *potentiae* he has been given. All find within man the potential for many actions. All demand action, which defines man. A man's life is his commitments plus his acts. This is all finite man can be.

The thinking of Karl Jaspers provides a model which may be more acceptable to today's existentially inclined counselors and therapists than Kierkegaard's "leap of faith" type of thinking.

Jaspers feels that it is a mark of maturity to live within an "unfinished" world view. However, the constant modern emphasis in philosophy on semantic analysis, objective science, and modern logic do not appear to him to be the way to know. Since man is constantly "becoming," since his "nature" is not fixed, man will always be more than he knows, more than he can know.

. . . life, self, mind, and matter are qualitatively different and . . . they cannot be reduced to any common term. In addition to the way of objective science and the way of metaphysics, there is the approach through an examination of personal existence. There are at least three areas to consider: man's consciousness . . . man's communication with his fellows . . . various historical structures of community life—morals, law, the family, the state.[30]

Jaspers feels that there are at least two selves in each person. One is the self able to be studied by psychology, the historically conditioned, biologically sensitive self. This self is responsive to the demands of the world around him, a creature of reflex and predictability. But the more "authentic self," as opposed to the previously described "empirical self," sometimes called the "transcendent self," is beyond the study of empirical methods and procedures. It is the source of meaning in life. This self makes possible life choices and freedom in face of severe environmental limiting factors possible.

This view of some aspect of self inaccessible to observation would be derided by the positivists as a type of flight from reality, a sort of personal entelechy subterfuge. Yet it is upon this point that the difference lies between the strict phenomenologist with his determinism and the existential phenomenologist or daseinanalyst with his *Dasein* vs. *Vorhandensein* modes of existence. It is a philosophical point of utmost importance to the therapist, the counselor, and the analyst.

From these necessarily brief considerations of the basic tenets of religious existentialists, several presuppositions can be seen:

1. A supreme God exists, a creating designer of the physical world, and the source of man's power to be and to act.

2. Mankind is becoming, has no fixed essence or nature. He makes himself what he will be within the limits of his *potentiae*. He can never know what these limits are, but through the process of decision and action, he can find satisfaction in living. God has not made man a creature of fixed nature; he must fashion himself by acts, commitments.

3. The dignity of each man is guaranteed by the awesome freedom which the all-knowing God saw fit to give him. He can preserve it by courageous action, or lose most of it by submerging himself in the collective, by being too afraid to walk his own road.

4. Willing, without action, is insignificant. Actions taken define man's essence. Existence precedes essence, and to some thinkers, essence is an illegitimate term. Man is what he does.

5. Choices are real; limitations exist (finiteness, physical surroundings, bodily limitations) but can be overcome by choice-plus-actions.

6. All mankind experiences the loneliness of being separated from God; man can seek comfort in his sufferings by involving himself in solacing others of his kind. He can spend his life making commitments which he deeply feels, and can aid others in their time of need.

The implications for counseling and guidance in the thinking of the religious existentialists will depend in large measure upon the particular brand of thought (i.e., the religious context in which one operates). However, in all these systems or concepts, it becomes clear that man's times of stress will come frequently. All of his daily problems and life choices can and should be viewed as part of his larger existential problem: finding meaning in life, a life which is contingent and which may come to an end at any time. This is not to say that all who come to a counselor with, for example, vocational problems or adjustment difficulties are keenly aware of this being-until-death. In fact, their very obliviousness to it may be part of the unrest and seeking-for-reassurance which the counselor sees every day. The *Daseinanalyse* approach attempts to view problems from inside the phenomenal structure, the personal meanings, of the client. He wants someone to share with him his own unique predicament. It is not enough to know that others have similar problems or the same problem, although this offers some solace to extremely naïve clients; he is alone, and unless someone can share his world of private meanings, he stays alone. This is often too much for the client in his existential anxiety to bear. He needs someone to "be with" him and "feel with" him in his deepest inner self, whatever the nature of that self might be.

Implications of Existentialist Thought for the Future of Guidance and Counseling

In his *Becoming*, Allport contrasted the thinking of two men whose philosophical and psychological successors have come to dominate the polar views in American psychology. He contrasted Locke's ideas of a *passive intellect* (which gave rise to S-R bond psychology, behaviorism, operationism, and reflex psychologies) with the *active intellect* posited by Leibniz. He contrasted the assumptions of the two outlooks.

LOCKEAN OUTLOOK

1. What is external and visible is more fundamental than what is not. Cause is external to the organism (a passive *tabula rasa*).
2. What is small and molecular (cf. Locke's "simple ideas") is more fundamental than what is large and molar (cf. Locke's "complex ideas"). The "habit unit" is of primary concern to psychologists of today.
3. Species equivalence is accepted strongly. Animals are taken as a prototype of humans. Allport quotes Hull: "Humans have the added capacity of speech, symbolic behavior, with the accompanying advantages of the higher mental processes. Whether this introduces any primary behavioral laws remains to be determined."

Allport states that these assumptions are congenial to positivism (e.g., that the devices employed in the experimentation of measurement shall be specified in the definitions of each concept). He points out that such reduction to observation data has led to concentration on areas which do lend themselves to such study. High level complexities have been little studied, perhaps because they cannot be specified with mathematical, positivistic precision.

LEIBNIZIAN OUTLOOK

1. The full-scale phenomenology which presupposes an active thinker and a primary process of relating this thinker to his own states of consciousness—represented in varying degrees by Brentano, Husserl, Scheler, and others—has led to a flourishing school of epistemology, but because of its inherent subjectivity has had little direct influence upon American psychology.
2. The Gestalt school, though directly influenced by this philosophical phenomenology, is grounded in the experimental tradition, and has led especially in Europe to a rich store of concepts that presume the existence of an *active intellect* (e.g., dynamical, self-distribution, belongingness, insight, closure). Unlike phenomenology proper, Gestalt theory does not place primary emphasis upon the subject-object relationship, but on varied, dynamic processes, each considered in its own right.
3. In American cognitive theory the concepts of Gestalt psychology have been considerably diminished so far as their emphasis upon self-activity (autochthonous process) is concerned, with the substitution of less dynamic concepts such as hypothesis, expectancy, cognitive maps.
4. Many American positivists and associationists repudiate all such conceptions, even the dilute American cognitive theory, and hold

that the conceptual frame of stimulus-response theory is adequate, and that the hypothesis of the "empty organism" is preferable to the assumption of an organism furnished with a self-active intellect.[31]

In condensed form, it becomes a matter of *active* organism vs. reactive organism. Those who conclude that they lean toward the active or "self-drive" view of man would, to the degree of their leaning, be followers of the Leibnizian tradition. Those who demand rigorous, objective, scientific measurement of and description of all phenomena would be, to the extent of their feelings, followers of Locke's tradition.

Although earlier writings in the field of guidance might be classified as pro-Lockean, the recent philosophical writings in the field of guidance have presented a faith in something more than a reactive organism. One need only read the writings of Wrenn, Rogers, Mathewson, and others mentioned in the more serious articles reviewed in Chapter Two to see this turning from the strictly deterministic phenomenology of the 1940's and early 1950's to modern meta-phenomenological direction which might be termed existential phenomenology or *Daseinanalyse*. If the analysis of this study is correct, then a whole new emphasis in counseling and counselor preparation is in store. This is not to discard the great scientific advances guidance has made in testing, etc. But certain presuppositions seem to imply a great many needed areas of study and conceptual revision.

The presuppositions now to be discussed are those of virtually all the leading existentialist writers, chiefly of Sartre. In the main they seem strongly in accord with various statements of Wrenn, Mathewson, Rogers, and others who have given serious philosophical thought to the guidance enterprise.

1. Man exists in a world of choices. Determinism is the basic fabric of the physical universe, but not of man.

2. Man must rely on himself and upon his fellow creatures to adjust to an adamant universe, or perish.

3. Values are names given or terms of praise or dissatisfaction which man assigns to events, things, or ideas which aid him or hinder him in existing.

4. Existence precedes essence. There is no Grand Plan into which all events must fit and to which all people "ought" to attune. Man *is;* he then evaluates himself and his world. He does not discover relationships; he creates them.

5. Man's physical existence is all he can know. This does not give him license, but rather casts upon him *responsibility* *to* *be* what his potential indicates *to* *him*.

6. Man's relationship to others must be that of self-realization for all, and creature comfort (empathy and sympathy) in living out the life-span confronting us all.

7. Loneliness is accepted as a fact of life. Longing is an attribute of man. Both can give rise to noble efforts to resist despair, or can lead to forlornness. Man chooses.

The eighth major presupposition is hardest for many to accept. There are both atheistic and theistic existentialists, as has been discussed in earlier paragraphs. Depending upon which orientation one chooses, item 8 will be accepted in rather different ways. It may be stated either that:

8. (a) There is no God, or (b) God created the world somewhat in the manner espoused by the eighteenth century deists (Paine, Franklin, and the French deists). The latter view is roughly that of the creating force which made the world, created man, and chose to leave him to his own devices, never or seldom to intervene again. Dogmatic religious persons, or those who for personal reasons cannot bear the thought of such a world may still accept what follows from these presuppositions by *justifying* procedures and ideas *on* *other* grounds. The presuppositions are clear.

If, as present guidance literature has indicated, the guidance enterprise is to come of age philosophically, a basic pattern of presuppositions seems necessary to establish guidelines, not just discussion of isolated ideas or debates on academic trappings to be used.

Let it be assumed for the moment that these assumptions be accepted by counselors, perhaps officially through their organizations.

The impact upon counselor training would be great. The philosophy of guidance would involve thorough study of existentialist ideas and assumptions followed by a relating of these to guidance activities. No longer would principles of guidance be only the presentation of "schools of thought" and specific problems which research has delved into to a degree.

Perhaps in a unified philosophical atmosphere, one which resolved or accommodated the various viewpoints, it might be possible to come up with an honest Credo for Counselors:

1. Every man, not mentally incompetent, is responsible for his acts.

2. Man can do little to change most of the physical universe, the

given, but he can predict it and make his life happier by facing reality.

3. Each man must aid others and try to understand their feelings, for mankind is left alone in an uncaring world.

4. Man creates his own nature. This is an individual choice.

5. Man should act toward others as he would want them to act toward him.

6. Decisions shall be made only by the criterion, "What is the effect on humankind?" Man must be treated with dignity; his status as a past-and-future-experiencing being, the only creature so endowed, makes this mandatory.

7. Determinism applies to physical laws; choice is a fact of human existence within the framework of the given surroundings.

8. Man counsels because no man can meet all problems alone.

9. Choices must be made by the counselee, for the counselor cannot claim omniscience.

10. The end of counseling is enabling fellow creatures better to bear the buffets of life, better to seek happiness and individual fulfillment.

11. Man must operate as if he is alone in the universe with his fellows; it is futile to argue about supernatural creation; there is no proof.

12. Man's suffering can be relieved by suggestions from those who have traveled the road before, or a road like it.

13. It would be an act of cruelty not to try to benefit others; they are involved with us in life.

The foregoing formulations are an attempt to reconcile the few, yet major, points of disagreement among counselors into a cohesive philosophical framework. The simple yet thoughtful philosophy of Sartre and the other existentialist writers seems to answer the situation.

Throughout all of the credo set forth above, one over-riding fact is clear: Man *needs* his fellows, deeply and vitally. They are his reference points in choosing, in groping for "reasons." It is a well-known fact that when a man dies, society provides a coroner, and spends money to determine a reason for dying; we must spend far more time and effort to determine a reason for living. This is the noblest aid that man can give to his fellow man.

Suggested Synthesis for the Future

Chapter Three demonstrated what have been and are the philosophical presuppositions of guidance. Some of these were shown to be at best awkward, tangential "agreements" and at their worst contradictory or tenuously explainable. The field of guidance must consolidate its presuppositions into some rubric, some frame of reference which will provide vital guidelines for the future.

The newer findings in the philosophy of existence and in the psychological insight of *Daseinanalyse* may provide this synthesis.

Inherent in the philosophy of existence is the doctrine of the responsibility of the individual for his own actions. This same belief was stated often in the literature of guidance as a fundamental rule of operation. For the sake of brevity, this and other apparent agreements of the basic ideas of guidance and of the philosophy of existence will be stated in the form of propositions which must be later explained, ramified, and defended.

PROPOSITION I: THE INDIVIDUAL IS RESPONSIBLE FOR HIS OWN ACTION. HE HAS A MEASURE OF CHOICE AND MUST MAKE SUCH CHOICES FOR HIMSELF.

In both guidance literature and in the philosophy of existence another theme recurred and seemed a necessary presupposition. It was that man has a stake in his society and in mankind as a whole. He has a responsibility to his fellows to act in a manner sympathetic to them; they are fellow commiserators on the existential journey. Man's chief hope for comfort and aid in his own decision making— his point of reference and point of comparison—was stated to be his fellow creatures.

PROPOSITION II. MAN MUST REGARD HIS FELLOWS AS OBJECTS OF VALUE, AS PART OF HIS OWN PROPRIUM. IF HIS FELLOWS ARE PART OF HIM, HE MUST APPLY THE RESPONSIBILITY MENTIONED IN PROPOSITION I TO ALL OF SOCIETY.

The common thread in the two propositions hinges upon the acceptance of the idea that, as Sartre and other existentialists of both religious and nonreligious persuasion have stated often, man must choose not only for himself, but for all mankind. This is strongly reminiscent of Kant's "practical imperative," the Christian Golden Rule, and the long tradition in the history of philosophy that man must of necessity become "his brother's keeper." There was no apparent disagreement in the literature reviewed with either of these two propositions. The whole enterprise of guidance has appeared to have rested upon these two premises; what follows would not *necessarily* follow were it not for such agreement.

PROPOSITION III: MAN EXISTS IN A WORLD OF REALITY. THE RELA-
TIONSHIP OF MAN TO HIS WORLD IS A THREATENING ONE, BECAUSE MUCH
OF WHAT HE ENCOUNTERS HE IS AT A LOSS TO CHANGE.

As has been stated, man is an existential creature. When man
ceases to exist, he can no longer be destroyed. While he exists, it is
with the full knowledge that at any time his existence can be brought
to an abrupt end. Poison in his purchased food, an automobile driver
gone berserk, a falling stone from a hillside, the chance striking of
a lightning bolt, the decision of war by others whom he does not
know and who do not know him—all these and countless others can
end his existence at a time he cannot predict. Proposition IV follows
from this third proposition.

PROPOSITION IV: A MEANINGFUL LIFE MUST REMOVE AS MUCH
THREAT FROM REALITY AS POSSIBLE, BOTH PHYSICAL AND PSYCHOLOGICAL.

It has already been stated that choice is a matter of basic assumption in the literature. The choice is circumscribed and limited by the
finiteness of man's organism, and the many forces which play upon
him. Nevertheless, man has the power and the responsibility to live
his own life in choices that are within his power. It follows that the
fewer and less powerful are the restricting forces, the wider the
limits of choice and of action, meaningful action. This proposition
provides the basis for concern about the welfare of ourselves and
others; for health services to combat disease (a destructive influence); for therapy—physical and verbal—to combat psychological
detriments that restrict the amount of reality individuals can see
clearly; for giving information about one's estimated potentials and
about reality (e.g., the world of work and its requirements). The
goal is to free man so that his optimum development can be obtained.
It must be stressed that even when others define the direction which
a client *might* take in reaching "optimum development" as they define it, they are fulfilling their responsibility: they are doing all they
can to free man. They are making their choices (as to method, estimation of his potential, and other factors) within the freedom that
their own life-space allows (e.g., their training, their own personal
beliefs gleaned from experience, their own field of influence), and
must then step into the background and let the client then assume
the ultimate responsibility for his own life decisions. Their object
is to help free him from obstacles, to remove threats for him so that
he might choose more wisely. They do this because they view him

as part of their proprium, as part of themselves in a generic sense. They may feel proud when man in the form of a client becomes self-activating once more, or when he becomes more "vital" in his outlook on life and living; they may feel sad or frustrated when he slips, when he remains less free. He is part of them.

The ultimate goal of counseling must be the freeing of the individual to make his choices, not to follow those made by "wiser" men. Following tentatively the insights of others might be necessary on the road toward independence and freedom, but the ultimate goal must be the independence. Propositions III and IV are entailed in each other just as are Propositions I and II. Both directive and nondirective positions agreed on the ultimate responsibility of the client to make his own decisions. The disagreement appeared to be in the ways to attain this with least loss of client time and effectiveness. The freeing of the client from the pressures of threatening situations was a goal of both. Both spoke of "developmental" aims, which ultimately meant that the client was aided to see his problems more clearly both at the time of stress and, by forming a pattern of approach, in the future.

PROPOSITION V: EVERY PERSON HAS HIS OWN HEREDITY AND HAS HAD EXPERIENCES UNIQUE UNTO HIMSELF. THEREFORE HE CAN BE EXPECTED TO REACT IN DIFFERENT WAYS FROM OTHER PEOPLE WHOSE LIFE-SPACE IS DIFFERENT.

The literature on individual differences and on phenomenology confirmed this and this point has not been questioned in the literature.

PROPOSITION VI: "OUGHT" IMPLIES "CAN," IF THE WORD "OUGHT" IS TO HAVE MEANING AT ALL IN HUMAN BEHAVIOR.

Linking Propositions V and VI, guidance must assume that *if* a person "behaves irrationally" or "cannot see reality" it is because he simply is not free in some important sense to behave otherwise at that given point in time. This is not contradictory with the statement that "people don't always do what they know is right." It is only to say that *if* someone knows and can perhaps verbalize what he ought to do and then does otherwise, there is some force acting upon him which makes this behavior *more* right, seen from his phenomenal perspective, than the point under discussion. If each person has had a unique life-space which has resulted in a particular set of personal values and strivings, as is presupposed in Proposition V, then it follows that no two people ever can see a situation in totally the same light. The very fact of their separate positions in time and space precludes this. It is the task of the counselor to try to understand as far as possible why one does other than what he professes to "know" he "ought" to do. He must know in advance that he can never know the client *in toto;* theoretically, to do so would be *to be* that client.

Just as no one person can know all the meanings and phenomena which effect and have effected his life—because of the finiteness of man—no counselor can know "the other" completely. Fortunately, it is not necessary that a given man know all the relationships in the past and present universe to live a full, satisfying life. Thus it is with counseling. The counselor need not know all of the personal meanings of the client to aid him in becoming free to live in his own life-style. Insofar as he can *approach empathy*, thus far can he make valid judgments as to what makes the client respond as he does to given life situations. Since men are somewhat similar because of their generic traits, and since the physical world is present to everyone, though differently viewed by us all, counselors can hypothesize and predict within rather well-defined limits what a client might be expected to do. As William James has warned us, however, "What ever the state of our knowledge of human behavior, biographies are not likely to be written in advance." There will be a margin of error. Some single influence or value might fly in the face of what might reasonably be expected; indeed the nature of this value or influence might never become known either to the counselor or to the counselee, but may have been an important determining factor. As stated in Proposition VI, it would be meaningless to state that a given person "ought" to do something if some factor in his experience made this physically or psychologically impossible. A more proper statement would have to be couched in less commanding terms; given the freedom to do X, man can reach a given goal by doing X. This takes the onus of mysticism and prescription from the "inherent" rightness of an act. It is seemingly more consistent with the facts of human experience. The commonly bandied "shoulds" and "oughts" have long been discussed by philosophers. Often a statement of "should" or "ought" can be shown to be merely an exhortative statement, no different significantly from "I like this" or "Do this." Once a goal is selected—and it is hoped that this selection is done by the client—there are logically consistent ways in which to approach the goal. But here again, there must be caution on the part of the counselor in trying to "move" the person toward the goal the client *says* he has chosen. The goal might be accepted as legitimate, attainable, and worthy by the counselor and may represent to the best of his knowledge the real goal of the client, but only the client knows why the goal has been selected; this is buried beneath the complex of his personal existence, and is known, perhaps, not even to himself.

PROPOSITION VII: IT IS POSSIBLE AND DESIRABLE TO COLLECT DATA SAMPLING TYPES OF BEHAVIOR FROM WHICH ACTUARIAL PREDICTIONS CAN BE MADE.

This was the basic presupposition on which the statistical, test-oriented phases of guidance and therapy were established.

PROPOSITION VIII: THE ACTUARIAL PREDICTION DERIVED FROM TESTING CAN OFTEN PROVE OF VALUE IN ESTIMATING OR PREDICTING BEHAVIOR OF HUMANS WHO SHARE CERTAIN TRAITS IN VARYING DEGREES.

All counselors readily admit that the percentage orientation and the margin of statistical error of tests and personality inventories must be taken into account when dealing with any given, unique human client, but the presupposition remains. In that it aids freeing man to act responsibly and wisely, it serves its purpose. The proposition stems from the presupposition that men possess behavior patterns which can be identified by sampling behavior and by carefully calculating the probable error due to the nature of the sample. If the test itself or the counselor's interpretation of it succeeds only in registering a "set" or prejudice or a misunderstanding in the client's field of existence, it has to that extent interfered with his freedom still further. Tests, therefore, cannot be given blanket condemnation or approval. Given the goal of freeing a particular human being from threat or insecure knowledge (also a threat), a test must be viewed as having contributed to that goal or not having contributed. We may call a test which apparently obviates the attainment of the goal "good," but for reasons of semantics a better expression is "effective," since this eliminates approbation or disapprobation, except in relation to a stated goal. It makes no statement as to the "social desirability" of that goal.

PROPOSITION IX: MAN REACTS AS A TOTAL ORGANISM TO ANY GIVEN SITUATION.

He cannot react either intellectually or emotionally to the exclusion of the other. His basic existential life-style or existential field is a whole; it cannot be totally separated. To the extent that man attempts to "compartmentalize himself," as May puts it, to that same extent does he become anxiety-filled, less free to develop and contribute to his own integrity patterns. If his reaction must be total and integrated in order that he might become free, it is incumbent upon the counselor to strive for such integration, and to aid his client to see goal-blocking compartmentalization, and to combat this.

PROPOSITION X: MAN CANNOT BE CLASSIFIED AS "GOOD" OR "EVIL" BY NATURE.

These words imply a criterion or criteria which are fraught with semantic difficulties. Given an objective, given a goal, the words can be used as meaningful terms of description or of approbation. Without an agreed-upon goal, they are meaningless or at best emotion-laden.

These basic presuppositions seem necessary if man is to aid his fellows in existing more effectively and happily. There are other presuppositions which will be stated later, but these basic ones need further discussion. How they have affected present-day guidance and the possibilities they hold in the light of recent psychological findings must be made clear.

Theological vs. Non-Theological Counselors

Cribbin's work repeatedly criticized the underlying assumptions in guidance as being too this-worldly and leaving out the "vital" assumption of a God whose creation of value-systems should be of prime concern to everyone.[32] The fact that his dissertation was written in a theologically oriented school, plus Cribbin's own religious conviction, might partly explain this view. However, seen from the standpoint of the synthesis proposed in this chapter, Cribbin's wishes cannot be written into guidance as a basic presupposition, since they do not fit all counselors. This split between those who feel that a First Presupposition or Supernatural Being must override all other considerations, and those who deny or at least have *not* agreed that such is a necessary presupposition, is difficult to reconcile if the older, traditional positions in philosophy are used as a model for guidance. However, the *Daseinanalyse* position finds room for both, just as existentialism could accommodate without contradiction the atheist Sartre and the religious Kierkegaard.

In Propositions I-X on the preceding pages there is no mention of whether God exists or whether there is a divine order of things, a Grand Plan. To the existentialist of the *Daseinanalyse* school this distinction makes no difference in human conduct. The ethical imperatives are the same; the commitment demanded is identical. If one can accept as desirable the basic tenets of *Daseinanalyse* thinking, it makes little difference what *else* he believes. His acceptance of these basic principles and belief will preclude the limiting of freedom, will assure the best efforts of each in aiding others. This is the strength of the *Daseinanalyse* approach in guidance. It is the reason, above all others, that precludes the adoption of some other model for the philosophy of guidance.

Returning to the questions of philosophy at the beginning of the chapter, the composite responses of those in guidance who accept the propositions just presented might be somewhat as follows:

Nature of Reality

The physical world exists and moves in accordance with predictable relationships. The methods of the sciences can formulate "laws" which describe (but not prescribe) and make possible predictions. Laws must be accepted as tentative, however, since the emerging nature of physical objects must necessarily leave a completed world view as only an approximation of existent reality. Man can, by his own decisions and acts, make himself into what he will be. No strict determinism applies to man's acts. (Whether the existential concept of no God or the religious existentialist idea of a deistic-type God is the basic premise, man's actions are to a great degree driven by a force within him.)

Man's Place in the Universe

Men are limited in their choices by finiteness and spatio-temporal location, but they are their own masters on this earth. Recognizing the human condition spoken of by Sartre and others, they *create* values (i.e., approve or disapprove of certain acts) which will further their genera. Starting from the basic presuppositions of man as determiner of his own actions, man learns that certain acts further freedom in himself and in others, certain acts enhance the dignity and physical-mental well-being of man. These acts he calls good, so long as they serve the purpose for which they are intended better than any other known acts. If man determines his individual essence as most existentialists state, "oughts" are not a priori universals; there is no room for this. "Oughts" are acts which are deeply felt to further the race of man and his existential amelioration.

Man is limited in what he can do by his organismic characteristics, by the causal-existential nature of his world, and by his own foreknowledge of his death. If he is to overcome to some degree tolerable to himself the gravity of his plight, he must count for something in terms of his deepest feelings. He must act, must commit himself to what he feels must be done.

His basic need from which all other needs stem is the need for God, for some designing force to aid him in life-choices. However, since this is not forthcoming, he seeks respite from his loneliness and feeling of forlornness. He seeks this respite by means of any activities which preserve and enhance his phenomenal self. It must be stressed that it is the phenomenal self which is to be preserved and enhanced, the self-as-perceived-by-self. This belief offers explanation of suicide, and acts of extreme heroism and self-sacrifice, for there are some conditions on earth which negate man's humanity, and are therefore less to be desired in certain situations than death-before-one's-time.

Nature of Knowledge

Knowledge is derived from past experience plus inference. The knowledge of physical events and "natural laws," if the term may be permitted in a descriptive sense only, can be obtained by the scientific methods of induction, by "hypothesis-test-correct hypothesis" method. On the level of physical events, man confirms his hypotheses by the degree to which they prove to enable him to predict future events. In that they do, they are valid. To the degree that they fail or are a bit inaccurate, to that degree are they deemed in need of correction.

The possession of knowledge does imply existential "oughts." If, as Sartre and others have stated, "Man chooses for all others in his acts," one who has come to have specialized knowledge must by actions use this knowledge to relieve so far as possible the anxieties, forlornness, and choice-difficulties of his fellows. The same applies to skills. If a skill possessed by a given man can make lighter the plight of his fellows, he is existentially immoral not to so use it.

Man and Freedom

Contrary to the phenomenological writings in guidance, man is free. This is at once a pleasant, heady luxury and also a source of his discontent. Man must shape himself and his world without an a priori right or wrong to guide him. Freedom implies causality in a very important sense. If the world, especially the physical world of objects around man, were indeterminate (i.e., capricious), no freedom could exist. Man could make no choices, for he would have no basis upon which to act. The world is viewed as having certain relatively stable relationships; within the bounds of these relatively stable limitations, man moves and lives. "Natural law" is not a prescription, but rather the statement (descriptive) of man's *present* knowledge of the physical world of realities. As man's new discoveries enlarge his frame of reference, he comes to richer conclusions, more predictability, and a better basis for choice-making.

Even in a closed-system universe, not all happenings would have an effect on all others. Indeed events of which individuals are not aware may play a great role in their life-styles, but to say that all events have a causal role in all others is tenuous and epiphenomenal. However, to say that only those events which are part of an individual's phenomenal field determine behavior is to maintain that events of which he is not conscious cannot effect behavior, or else a tautology is necessary, as has been shown in Chapter Three.

At man's present stage of knowledge there is no evidence to believe that *all* physical happenings are purpose-fulfilling, or if so, they are in countless cases so remote from the lives of men as to be of little value to him in his existential plight. Certain predictable events can be *used* for man's purposes, but they are not in and of themselves purpose-fulfilling.

A supernatural world is viewed differently by the atheistic and the theistic existentialist. However, both feel that whether God exists or not, man is left to his own devices in this life. The happenings in this world can be explained parsimoniously without reference to a supernatural realm. Some of the literature in counseling makes references to such a realm and to Divine Will, etc., but this has not been carried over into necessary or sufficient guidance practices. If one chooses to make the "leap of faith" embraced by Kierkegaard, he will still be faced with the daily feelings of his nonaccepting fellows, the human anxieties, the necessity for constant choice-making in his life.

Worth, Good, Evil

The only absolutes, if they may be termed such, in existentialist thought are freedom and dignity of the individual. They are necessary presuppositions for his whole life-style. There are for him no other guidelines than these plus his own power to infer his course of action in furthering them. People must be treated as ends, not as means, yet there will arise situations in which some people must suffer if many others are to exist at all. The hierarchy of values ultimately must be derived from one's own inner commitments and past experiences in trying to further freedom and dignity, and inferences from these. Because certain elements of human experience are common to all men in a given culture, men will come to value in somewhat the same way. The evolution of law and religio-ethical systems is a case in point. But even law must be interpreted. Broad guidelines are provided by cultural heritage, but the ultimate decisions of life must be faced by each man who must then accept responsibility for his decisions. One is reminded here of a lyric in a hymn:

> Jesus walked the lonesome valley,
> He had to walk it by Himself;
> For nobody else would walk it for Him—
> He had to walk it—all by Himself.[33]

Man finds himself in the same plight. Whether one is religious or irreligious, he must in some way face up to his life. His life and the meaning of it are recorded in his actions. Perhaps the chief difference in the two types of existentialists on the level of living is that one is walking his "lonesome valley" with no knowledge of the terrain, except what he can see and from what his fellows, traveling their own "lonesome valleys," tell him in a spirit of mutual aid and sympathy. The other, the religious existentialist, has a chart or map of the terrain to aid him in moving onward; he is constantly in fear, however, that the map he has been given may not be authentic; he has seen other maps which are different. He travels on, looking at the map, but making his decisions himself. A map points a direction, but it does not say when to walk fast, when to rest, or when to leave the trail to avoid unexpected debris which threatens the traveler.

Mandatory Goals

There are no mandates under existentialism, only the warning that *man is* what he *does*, and nothing more. From the presuppositions presented earlier in this dissertation, especially those involving freedom and concern for all men, it would follow that *not* all goals are equally worthwhile (e.g., enslavement of a group of men for the material advantage of the conquerors). Differences in choices made are understandable; men differ in their ability to accept the responsibility for "choosing for all men." But this does not ennoble their chosen goal; slavery in any form negates freedom, negates human dignity. The existentialist fights against all forms of it.

If by "responsibility" one means pre-existent commands to be obeyed or a master plan to be fulfilled, it is indeed a meaningless term in existentialist thought. But if it is a term denoting empathy, sympathy, and genuine free action in "choosing for all men," it is a vital word to the existentialist. It governs all his actions. Again, because of common symbols in the experience of men, especially those of one culture, there will be available a consensus by which one may "check" his feelings for validity, but in the ultimate analysis he must choose. Ethical situations have the unpleasant habit of being neither wholly black nor white. Man must make his own decisions and act.

These are the existentialist responses to the questions of general philosophy, albeit brief ones. From these can be deduced and debated the answers of courses of action for counseling. *Dasein-analyse*, existentialist counseling, existential phenomenology, existential therapy, and combinations of these provide new frameworks for the study of mankind. Nowhere is Pope's classic statement more apropos than in the philosophy of guidance: "The proper study of mankind is man."

The Existentialist would add, ". . . individual man!"

This might well be the touchstone for the education of counselors. Since the education of those who will do the bulk of the counseling in our schools and elsewhere is so important, perhaps it would be well in closing to speculate what implications the recent existentialist influences in therapy and in counseling might have in the training of counselors.

Proposal I: All counselors might well receive a course or series of courses entitled "Philosophy of Guidance," or be required to study an introductory course plus one in existentialism before completion of counselor training.

Proposal II: Leading theorists in the field of guidance might well make a serious examination of general and existential philosophy. These are the men who can make the greatest contribution to the literature and to the training of counselors. If that training is to be in depth consonant with the seriousness of the enterprise, it would seem that this might be a logical starting point. Indeed, Proposition II may prove to be a *sine qua non* for Proposition I, for merely adding a course to a curriculum solves nothing unless it is vital and meets a real deficiency.

Proposal III: In-service study groups might be formed to study the pertinent writings mentioned in this book and listed in the Appendix. All the talk of setting up a "position" in philosophy of guidance will go for naught unless those in the field reap the benefit of the systematic school of thought deduced from the past literature, current demands, and challenges to guidance.

Proposal IV: Symposium study of the new currents in existential thought as applied to counseling—involving the leaders in the field plus philosophers interested in the problems of psychology— might prove of great value in guiding the thinking of counselors.

Proposal V: Publication—jointly—by philosophers of psychology and by guidance authorities of a journal dealing with the philosophy of guidance. This might reduce the great deficiency of philosophical analysis noted in the literature. A tentative title might be *Philosophy of Guidance* (or *Counseling*) *Quarterly*. If this could not be done, perhaps a *Yearbook in the Philosophy of Guidance*, written jointly by philosophers and guidance experts, might serve well.

Footnotes

[1] Henry Borow, "The Logic of Counseling Research," *Journal of Counseling Psychology*, Vol. 4 (1956), 292-98.

[2] Harold Pepinsky, "Research Notes from Here and There," *Journal of Counseling Psychology*, Vol. 3 (1956), 222-28.

[3] Leona Tyler, "Minimum Change Therapy," *Personnel and Guidance Journal*, Vol. 38 (1960), 475-79.

[4] Edna Harrison, "The Counselor's Role in the Early Identification of Gifted Children," *Personnel and Guidance Journal*, Vol. 9 (May 1961), 735-37.

[5] B. Paul Komisar, "The Pedagogical Concept of Need," Unpublished mimeographed paper obtained from Dr. Robert H. Beck of the University of Minnesota in 1959. This later appeared in B. O. Smith and R. H. Ennis, *Language and Concepts in Education* (Chicago: Rand McNally Company, 1961).

[6] Donald Snygg, "The Need for a Phenomenological System in Psychology," *Psychological Review*, Vol. 48 (1941), 404-24. Reported in A. Kuenzli, *The Phenomenological Problem* (New York: Harper & Row, Publishers, 1959).

[7] Donald Snygg, *op. cit.*, 23-24.

[8] Edward Dreyfus, "Counseling and Existentialism," *Journal of Counseling Psychology* (Summer 1962), pp. 128-32.

[9] Carl Rogers, "The Way To Do Is To Be: A Review of *Existence*" (by May), *Contemporary Psychology*, Vol. 4 (1959), 196-98.

[10] Rollo May, *Existence* (New York: Basic Books, Inc., 1958), p. 37.

[11] *Ibid.*, p. 38.

[12] Robert F. Creegan, "Phenomenology," *Encyclopedia of Psychology*, ed. Philip Harriman (New York: The Citadel Press, 1951), p. 512.

[13] May, *op. cit.*, p. 78.

[14] Rollo May, *op. cit.*, p. 82. Taken from C. Rogers, "Persons or Science? A Philosophical Question," *American Psychologist*, Vol. 10 (1955), 267-78.

[15] Harold H. Titus, *Living Issues in Philosophy* (New York: American Book Company, 1946), p. 292.

[16] J. P. Sartre, *Existentialism*, trans. Bernard Frectman (New York: Philosophical Library, 1947), pp. 3-4.

[17] *Ibid.*, p. 15.

[18] *Ibid.*, p. 18-19

[19] *Ibid.*, p. 19-20.

[20] *Ibid.*, p. 25.

[21] *Ibid.*, p. 26-27.

[22] *Ibid.*, p. 27.

[23] *Ibid.*, p. 32.

[24] *Ibid.*, p. 45-46.

[25] *Ibid.*, pp. 28-29.

[26] *Ibid.*, p. 91.

[27] *Loc. Cit.*

[28] Titus, *op. cit.*, p. 295.

[29] Titus, *op. cit.*, p. 296.

[30] Titus, *op. cit.*, p. 301.

[31] Gordon Allport, *Becoming* (New Haven: Yale University Press, 1955).

[32] James Cribbin, *An Analysis of the Theological, Philosophical, Psychological and Sociological Principles of Guidance Presented in Textbooks Published Since 1935.* Unpublished Doctoral Dissertation (New York: Fordham University, 1951).

[33] A spiritual from the southern United States.

CHAPTER FIVE

❖ Summary and Conclusions of Philosophical Presuppositions of Guidance

The frequent statements in guidance-personnel literature calling for examination and clarification of the philosophy or philosophies of guidance indicated that the analysis of philosophical presuppositions was clearly a legitimate part of the literature.

The actions of those agents of society who have performed the functions of guidance-personnel work throughout history have been governed by presuppositions which have been identified. The presuppositions have been closely tied to the social system in which the agents functioned. The presuppositions of one time and place have been different from those in other settings.

The formal development of guidance was chiefly American, and had its beginnings in the late nineteenth century.

Most prominent among the presuppositions of guidance in America was a commitment to a democratic form of society rather than to an authoritarian form. Also prominent were the descriptions of the healthy personality, which included traits deemed desirable in a democracy: productive, healthy, self-governing, cooperative, socially efficient, ethically sensitive.

Guidance and personnel work has been recommended as one major step toward alleviating interpersonal, intergroup, and intercultural conflicts.

The literature sometimes stated, more often implied, a naturalistic world view. This was expressed in "this-worldly" objectives for education and in statements about the nature of man. Some writers spoke of spiritual values, Divine Will, and statements of counseling theory belied this; nothing in the literature seemed necessarily to translate this supernatural goal-seeking into counselor behavior.

Although change was discussed as the basic fabric of the universe, the ontological concept which was accepted, knowingly or un-knowingly, was that of a relatively stable world which could be known. Until only recently the basic test of truth was the corre-spondence theory of truth. The literature has stated faith in the instrumentalist consensus criteria, but this was a tentative, superficial agreement; consensus was used until, and only until, there was agree-ment as to what the objective "facts" of a given situation "really are." This was true of both clinical and nondirective counseling, of religious and nonreligious counseling.

Cause-and-effect relationships were presupposed, in keeping with what appeared to be a neo-realist "working position" of the major writers in guidance. Field theory was embraced as a frame of refer-ence in the early 1950's, although its present-centeredness caused some difficulties among theorists. Many of the neo-Freudian schools still prefer to stress the past as the main determiner of the future, rather than one's present field of forces.

In the late 1950's the spotlight turned to the phenomenological frame of reference. Wrenn, Rogers, and Patterson, to name only three leading examples, subscribed closely to the basic phenomeno-logical outlook as stated most distinctly by Snygg and Combs. This position caused logical and other difficulties, since phenomenology as described by Snygg and Combs is deterministic, while Rogers and others previously and subsequently have acted upon the presuppo-sition of a large measure of free will, upon the presupposition that choice is more than an illusion. This apparent contradiction needs further clarification from the authors who have embraced the phe-nomenological outlook, yet cling to choice and free will as basic to their views of guidance. The insights of the *Daseinanalyse* move-ment in psychotherapy may provide room for both views, but semantic differences must be made clear and agreements in mean-ings must be reached.

While many statements were found in the literature about indi-vidual value systems and individual valuing, an axiological realism appeared to be the ultimate belief of nearly all writers in the field, including the nondirectives. Here again, in matters of ethical, social, and aesthetic judgments, group consensus was not the final word, but was rather the first step in checking hypotheses. The final criterion was the matching of the hypotheses with reality, with the hope that all reasonable men would see things as they "really are." The consensus was not the basic criterion here, but rather the faith that, given the objective test of several judges or observers, the correspondence theory of truth would guide them in seeing the truth. This was the most troublesome point of view in the literature in regard to aligning guidance with instrumentalism. Several leading writers stated that guidance operates on the premises of instrumentalism or experimentalism, but this agreement was not found when basic presuppositions were examined. Guidance apparently does not at present grant the relativism in values that is necessary for the instrumentalist position, nor does it allow for the ontological concept of change necessary to the experimentalist. The tests of truth have been different: workability and consensus for the experimentalist, correspondence with pre-existent reality for the realist and, apparently, for the leading writers in guidance. Neo-realism appeared to be the philosophical position upon which modern guidance was founded. The neo-realist position of several writers in general philosophy seemed to fit the beliefs and practices of guidance (viz., Edwin Holt, W. P. Montague, E. G. Spaulding, and Walter Marvin). Their positions rejected the view that things (objects) are created, modified, or otherwise altered by the act of cognition alone. There is an outer world (sometimes called "real" world) which man experiences through his senses, and through his senses only. The common objects of experience, their relationships to each other, and their qualities seem quite insensitive to man's having experienced them or not. After man becomes aware of the objects of his experience, he may *then* alter the situation (e.g., by damming a river after he sees a need to do so), *but the action of cognition alone does not* create or change the world objects. The axiological views of this position have been discussed herein and appear to fit well the axiological presuppositions of guidance writers.

The epistemological presupposition most prominent in the literature was that truth is not reached through problem-solving or consensus, but rather by checking the hypotheses against the world "out there": its harsh requirements, its rewards for various actions, the reliability of a given "fact." The test was scientific verification and inductive logic, rather than consensus and deductive logic.

Knowledge was deemed valid insofar as the predictive statements made were verified or, perhaps more important, verifiable in experience, through the methods of science. Chief among these methods were measurement, testing of alternatives, and controlled observation.

All writers appeared to agree that the end of guidance and of the processes of guidance was not problem-solving alone, but more fundamentally an aid to self-guidance and to personal development, which meant ultimately the congruence of the person's phenomenological field with "objective reality." Maladjustment was considered symptomatic of non-congruence.

A difficulty arises if the world is viewed ontologically as a deterministic one, since one of the basic constructs of almost all of the writers was some form of "self-starter" within the organism (e.g., Rogers' idea of a "force driving one toward adjustment"). This concept appeared not to be verifiable even in principle, and from the neo-realist's epistemological point of view, therefore, would not logically be admitted as knowledge.

Determinism seemed to be a strong presupposition in all schools of counseling and guidance theory, even in field theory of Lewin's type. If one's life-space consists of X number of variables and, hence Y vectors, free choice can be considered no more than an illusion. Unless one postulates a supernatural phenomenon, unbound by the natural forces and fields, choice becomes fiction. One's actions under field theory are merely the direction determined by his field of forces.

If choice is a fiction and if determinism is the ontological fabric of the universe, there can be neither praise nor blame for human actions. "Ought" implies "can" to the philosopher of the neo-realist school; if one *cannot* do otherwise, "ought" becomes an empty word. If one is in the control of forces outside his power to change, he is not "responsible" for his actions. If there is no "responsibility" possible in the world, several questions in guidance become difficult to answer (e.g., what reason for existence has disciplinary counseling?). These questions must be faced by those who embrace either field theory or phenomenology.

Ethical standards were thought to pre-exist along with all other value judgments (i.e., were there to be discovered whether men in fact did discover them or not), and all "reasonable" men, if they applied the methods of inductive logic and of science, could come to know them (congruence with reality), thereby agreeing on what such standards are. Even nondirective theorists have aimed for this same congruence, but have laid heavier emphasis on reason than on the scientific apparatus (e.g., testing) used by the more directive or clinical types of counseling.

"Intuition" was mentioned fairly often in the literature by name or by the phrase "direct experiencing of the client's problem." This idea is incompatible with the presupposition that science is the method of finding truth. Sensory experiencing is the reception process in the neo-realist philosophy; the "experiencing somehow directly" which was spoken of in guidance seemed to negate the idea that *all* data must be received through the senses. There is, of course, the as yet unproven possibility that "intuition" is in fact a "sixth sense" which has some empirical basis, as many modern fiction writers have suggested. Until proven, however, this remains a seemingly illegitimate source of knowing. Much that is ascribed to intuition can be explained, perhaps, in naturalistic terms revolving about incompletely formed hypotheses, subconscious "adding up" of subliminal factors, or other naturalistic phenomena. "Intuition" may be no more than an unconscious or semiconscious ordering of events which approaches the Gestalt phenomenon of "closure."

The often-mentioned "change," which is the basis for many statements that guidance is properly an instrumentalist- or experimentalist-oriented enterprise, can be explained parsimoniously by viewing man's *experiencing* of the world as the thing changing, not the world itself. At any given point in time and space one views things and values differently, for he has not (because of his finiteness and his "positioning") "seen the picture whole," has not reached a complete congruence with reality. As he moves toward congruence with reality, he states that *it* has changed, much in the same manner as a child feels that the telephone poles are moving when he rides a train.

Spiritual values were mentioned sporadically in the literature, especially in the writings of the acknowledged leaders in the field, but no evidence appeared in the research or in stated *modus operandi* which indicated that these phenomena were *necessary* to guidance.

Spiritual values could be reconcilable with present practices and theories, but the principle of parsimony would make this seem either irrelevant or unnecessary for carrying out guidance activities. Dissent (in dismissing as unnecessary the "spiritual" phase of guidance) would, of course, come from the theistically oriented counselors such as Brady and Cribbin. There are others, too, who—while defining the term "spiritual" in a non-theistic manner (deistic, humanistic)—might also feel that guidance "loses something" when this assumption is made. Such dissenters have proposed theories of proximate ends and ultimate ends to reconcile theories of both "positivists" and "theists" in guidance.

Also in evidence in the literature was a social determinism arising from man's striving to move closer to pre-existent reality and values. As he approaches congruence through the methods of science, there appears to be little choice as to "social direction," for as Rogers has described the situation, "all reasonable men will then come to hold values having great similarity with all others."

This social determinism which follows from the presuppositions apparent in the literature is of great import. Some may look to it as a type of salvation, as an end to the fighting and bickering of mankind caused by differences in value and ends; others may envision a "set society" in which all think alike and which will suppress novelty and progress.

Modern guidance, then, may be described philosophically as man's attempt to discover the pre-existent truths about himself, his world, and the world of values (all relationship-determined) by the methods of science and inductive logic, and to aid others in pursuing these goals by sharing insights gained with those who have not attained the same degree of congruence with reality.

The seemingly irreconcilable rift between the theologically oriented guidance theorists and the science-stressing guidance theorists can be reduced to (a) agreement that objective reality and a realist-type world view do prevail and (b) disagreement, or at least a lack of communication, as to the source, naturalistic or theistic, of these values and objects.

Phenomenology, and usually of the brand indicated by Snygg and Combs, appeared at variance with the basic assumptions of choice in guidance. Further explanation is needed by leading guidance theorists who have embraced phenomenology as a "new direction in guidance" while still clinging to the presupposition of choice in man's world.

The points of friction between those now embracing the phenomenological explanation of human behavior, yet dissatisfied with the lack of choice which follows from it, may find unity with the philosophy of existence and with the insights of *Daseinanalyse* psychology. Both of these are extensions of phenomenology, yet encompass qualities of human existence which many guidance writers have said they "feel," yet cannot explain in terms of theory. The points of friction between the metaphysical feelings of these writers and the neo-realist presuppositions under which guidance has been operating seem unable to be reconciled by any known philosophy except existentialist thought and *Daseinanalyse* psychology.

The fundamental presuppositions of guidance at present may be stated as:

1. An objective order of physical reality exists, independent of the knower, unaffected by the act of cognition.

2. Causality and regularity apply to both physical objects and human actions, although these are complex.

3. Human organisms have an organization of potentialities (possibilities) which remain relatively stable throughout life, "differentiating" and "weakening or strengthening" rather than "changing" in a genuinely ontological sense.

4. Man can know only what is inside his phenomenal field; even inferences are made on the basis of the organization of his field.

5. Understanding a client precedes assisting him.

6. Empathy is possible because of the common meanings due to culture and common objects of experience. It cannot be total, but need not be.

7. Determinism is at present accepted as the framework of nature. Man infers this from the fact that he has found much lawfulness, and seeks more.

8. Each organism has the potential to solve his own life's problems if only the obstacles to seeing them clearly can be pointed out.

9. Each individual must, in the final analysis, make his own "choices" and must assume responsibility for his decisions. (This presupposition is often found in the literature, but does not fit the description of human behavior found in phenomenology.)

10. The dignity and worth of the individual, and his right to pursue his own life-style, is presupposed. The democratic form of government is often mentioned as most consonant with this end.

11. Guidance is concerned with the "optimum development" of each man's (presupposed) potentialities. (This statement is semantically difficult, unless the *Daseinanalyse* thinking is employed.)

12. Organisms react as a whole; the total life-space of an individual must be taken into account in counseling.

13. "Change" is apparently *not* a presupposition, but a confusion in meaning stemming from the early history of guidance. "Dynamic transition" is here offered to express the intended meaning of "constantly restructured fields, but not *irreversibly* restructured."

14. Correspondence with truth or reality is the test of knowledge claims. Since the restructuring of fields is constantly taking place, man cannot see reality "whole." Therefore, the nearest approximation to truth is the consensus of "qualified observers," a difficult but necessary concept.

15. Inference made on the basis of past experiences constitutes a useful tool in making predictions in the lawful, "closed system" universe.

16. Inference is the only source of knowledge. Even "new" experiences are accepted into the field of the observer via a restructuring process.

17. "Intuition," mentioned several times in the literature, can be explained naturalistically in terms similar to the Gestalt "closure" phenomenon.

18. Naturalism is the ontological concomitant of phenomenology; supernaturalism is excluded as non-parsimonious.

19. The individual has "needs" which represent the actions necessary to maintain and/or enhance his phenomenal self. (This concept remains tautological unless a new framework for guidance such as existentialist philosophy is adopted.)

20. Freeing the individual to make his own choices is proposed frequently, but this is anomaly under phenomenology. Choice is an illusion under the phenomenological system. It is here proposed that this presupposition might be stated as "Restructuring the field of the client who comes for help, so that his *backlog* of experiences, attitudes and meanings *available for dealing with future problems will grow.*"

21. Any means of studying the client, thereby enabling the counselor to restructure the field in the direction of the client's goals, is permissible *if* such method does not infringe upon other areas of the client's life which he values more than the particular goals under discussion.

22. There are optimum ways of behaving which society approves as preserving itself and keeping "social equilibrium" intact. (This is fundamentally a macrocosmic version of the individual behavior model of phenomenology.) A reasoning organism can come to

know these ways of behaving and will accept them *if* he is freed from the "barriers" to seeing them objectively.

Presuppositions 9, 10, 11, 15, and 18 do not admit of easy proof. Research has not dealt with these presuppositions to any degree, and perhaps cannot. Deductive discussion could be employed to approximate justification, however. All of the above can be accepted and assimilated into existentialist philosophy and *Daseinanalyse* psychology. The present neo-realist orientation of guidance cannot logically accept all of these presuppositions from the literature.

Recent statements in the literature, new developments in European psychology, and the demands from the literature for certain types of research indicate that neo-realism is not a broad enough framework for the future of guidance, and that instrumentalism also is inadequate. It has been herein proposed that existentialist philosophy and *Daseinanalyse* theory can provide the needed framework for the future.

❖ Bibliography

PART I

Adams, Arthur S., "How Shall One Find His Way?" *Educational Record*, Vol. 29 (Apr. 1942), 104-109.

Allport, Gordon, *Becoming*. New Haven: Yale University Press, 1955.

American Council on Education, Committee on Student Personnel Work, *The Student Personnel Point of View*, rev. ed. Studies Series 6, No. 13. Washington, D.C.: The Council, 1949.

American Personnel and Guidance Association, "A Statement of Policy: Standards for the Preparation of School Counselors," *Personnel and Guidance Journal*, Vol. 4 (Dec. 1961), 402-407.

Arbuckle, Dugald, "Counseling: Philosophy or Science?" *Personnel and Guidance Journal*, Vol. 39 (Sept. 1960), 11-14.

————, "Five Philosophical Issues in Counseling," *Journal of Counseling Psychology*, Vol. 5 (Fall 1958), 211-15.

————, *Student Personnel Services in Higher Education*. New York: McGraw-Hill Book Company, Inc., 1953.

Barry, Ruth, and Beverly Wolf, *Modern Issues in Guidance-Student Personnel Work*. New York: Teachers College, Columbia University, 1957.

Benezet, Louis T., "Guidance in Moral and Spiritual Values," *Counseling and Guidance in General Education*, ed. Melvene Hardee, pp. 73-79. Yonkers, N.Y.: World Book Company, 1955.

Benjamin, Harold R., "The Poverty of Nations," *Personnel and Guidance Journal*, Vol. 35 (Nov. 1956), 140-44.

Berger, Emanuel, "Zen Buddhism, General Psychology and Counseling Psychology," *Journal of Counseling Psychology*, Vol. 4 (Summer 1962), 122-27.

Bordin, Edward S., Jr., "A Counseling Psychologist Views Personality Development," *Journal of Counseling Psychology*, Vol. 4 (Spring 1957), 3-8.

————, *Psychological Counseling*. New York: Appleton-Century-Crofts, 1955.

————, "Student Personnel Work and Personality Development," *Personnel and Guidance Journal*, Vol. 33 (Dec. 1954), 194-98.

Borow, Henry, "The Logic of Counseling Research," *Journal of Counseling Psychology*, Vol. 4 (1956), 292-98.

Brady, Dominic, O.P., *An Analytical Study of Counseling Theory and Practice with Recommendations for the Philosophy of Counseling*. Washington, D.C.: Catholic University Press, 1952.

Brammer, Lawrence, and Everett Shostrom, *Therapeutic Psychology: Fundamentals of Counseling and Psychotherapy*. Englewood Cliffs, N.J.: Prentice-Hall, Inc., 1960.

Brown, Dirck, "Interpreting the College Student to Prospective Employers, Government Agencies, and Graduate Schools," *Personnel and Guidance Journal*, Vol. 7 (Mar. 1961), 576-82.

Brown, F., "Identifying College Drop-Outs with the Minnesota Counseling Inventory," *Personnel and Guidance Journal*, Vol. 39 (1960), 280-82.

Brown, Robert W., "The Teacher as a Guidance Worker," *Journal of Education*, Vol. 139 (Apr. 1957), 3-12.

Browning, R. L., and H. J. Peters, "On the Philosophical Neutrality of Counselors," *Educational Theory* (Apr. 1960).

Cannom, Charles W., "Philosophical Principles," in Brouwer's *Student Personnel Services in General Education*, pp. 275-77. Washington, D.C.: American Council on Education, 1949.

Cantril, Hadley, "Perception and Interpersonal Relations," *The American Journal of Psychiatry*, Vol. 114 (1957), 119-26.

Combs, Arthur, "Counseling as a Learning Process," *Journal of Counseling Psychology*, Vol. 1 (Winter 1954), 31-36.

————, and Daniel W. Soper, "The Self, Its Derivative Terms, and Research," *Journal of Individual Psychology*, Vol. 13 (1957), 134-45.

Crawford, Albert B., and Stuart H. Clement, *The Choice of an Occupation*. New Haven: Yale University Press, 1959.

Cribbin, James J., *An Analysis of the Theological, Philosophical, Psychological, and Sociological Principles of Guidance Presented in Textbooks Published Since 1935*. New York: Fordham University, 1951. Taken from a doctoral dissertation of the same title which contained 462 pages exclusive of bibliography.

————, "Critique of the Philosophy of Modern Guidance," *Catholic Educational Review*, Vol. 53 (Feb. 1955), 73-91.

——, "The Modern Function of Guidance—an Ancient Christian Tradition," *Catholic Educational Review*, Vol. 52 (Nov. 1954), 510-22.

Cronbach, L. J., *Essentials of Psychological Testing*, 2nd ed. New York: Harper & Row, Publishers, 1960.

Curran, Charles A., "Guidance and Counseling in Education," *Education*, Vol. 73 (Dec. 1952), 223-28.

——, "Some Ethical and Scientific Values in the Counseling Therapeutic Process," *Personnel and Guidance Journal*, Vol. 39 (Sept. 1960), 15-20.

Drake, William, *The American School in Transition*. Englewood Cliffs, N.J.: Prentice-Hall, Inc., 1955.

Dressel, Paul, "The Determination of Student Needs," *Counseling and Guidance in General Education*, ed. Melvene Hardee, pp. 26-46. Yonkers, N.Y.: World Book Company, 1955.

Dreyfus, Edward, "Counseling and Existentialism," *Journal of Counseling Psychology*, Vol. 9 (Summer 1962), 128-32.

Dugan, Willis, ed., *Counseling Points of View: Proceedings of Mid-Winter Conference, 1958*. Minneapolis: University of Minnesota Press, 1959.

Durnall, Edward J., Jr., James F. Moynihan, and C. G. Wrenn, "Symposium: The Counselor and His Religion," *Personnel and Guidance Journal*, Vol. 36 (Jan. 1958), 326-34.

Farwell, Gail, and Herman Peters, *Guidance Readings for Counselors*. Chicago: Rand McNally & Company, 1960.

Fisher, Margaret, and Robert Roth, "Structure: An Essential Framework for Research," *Personnel and Guidance Journal*, Vol. 8 (Apr. 1961), 639-44.

Ford, E., *et al.*, "Psychotherapy with Child Psychotics," *American Journal of Psychotherapy*, Vol. 14 (1960), 705-18.

Froehlich, Clifford P., "Stars, Parsons and Clients," *Personnel and Guidance Journal*, Vol. 36 (Sept. 1957), 10-16.

Fromm, Florence, "New Approaches to Counseling and Discipline," *Journal of the National Association of Women Deans and Counselors*, Vol. 20 (Oct. 1956), 31-32.

Ginsberg, Eli, "Guidance—Limited or Unlimited," *Personnel and Guidance Journal*, Vol. 9 (May 1960), 707-12.

Glanz, Edward, "Emerging Concepts and Patterns of Guidance in American Education," *Personnel and Guidance Journal* (Nov. 1961), 259-65.

Gruen, Walter, "The Utilization of Creative Potential in Our Society," *Journal of Counseling Psychology*, Vol. 1 (Spring 1962), 79-83.

Hagmaier, George, and Robert Gleason, *Counseling the Catholic: Modern Techniques and Emotional Conflicts*. New York: Sheed & Ward, Inc., 1959.

Hall, Robert, and Joseph Lauwerys, eds., *Yearbook of Education, 1955: Guidance and Counseling.* Yonkers, N.Y.: World Book Company, 1955

Hardee, Melvene, "Moral Guidance, Our Responsibility," *Personnel and Guidance Journal,* Vol. 31 (Jan. 1953), 220-23.

Harrison, Edna L., "The Counselor's Role in the Early Identification of Gifted Children," *Personnel and Guidance Journal,* Vol. 9 (May 1961), 735-37.

Hiltner, Seward, "Counseling Viewed as a Part of the Educational Process," *Religious Education,* Vol. 51 (Nov. 1956), 414-15.

Hitchcock, Arthur A., "Milestones in the Development of Personnel Services in Education," *Student Personnel Services in Education,* Fifty-eighth Yearbook of the National Society for the Study of Education, Part II. Chicago: University of Chicago Press, 1959.

Hobbs, N., "Science and Ethical Behavior," *The American Psychologist,* Vol. 14 (1959), 217-25.

Hummel, Raymond, "Vocational Development Theory and Guidance Practice," *Journal of the National Association of Deans of Women,* Vol. 18 (Oct. 1954), 13-18.

Hutson, Percival, "The Rationale of Guidance," *Bulletin of the National Association of Secondary-School Principals,* Vol. 42 (Mar. 1958), 121-28.

Jourard, Sidney M., *Personal Adjustment, An Approach Through the Study of Healthy Personality.* New York: The Macmillan Company, 1958.

Kelman, Norman, "Psychoanalysis and Morality," *American Scholar,* Vol. 24 (Spring 1955).

Kitson, Harry D., "Psychology in Vocational Adjustment," *Personnel and Guidance Journal,* Vol. 36 (Jan. 1958), 314-19.

Kneller, George F., "Worldly View of Guidance and Counseling," *Journal of Higher Education,* Vol. 27 (Mar. 1956), 158-65.

Komisar, B. Paul, "The Pedagogical Concept of Need." Unpublished mimeographed paper, 1959.

Lee, Dorothy, "Individual Autonomy and Social Structure," *Personnel and Guidance Journal,* Vol. 35 (Sept. 1956), 16-21.

Leonard Eugenie, *Origins of Personnel Services in American Higher Education.* Minneapolis: University of Minnesota Press, 1956.

Levine, L. S., and R. Kantor, "Psychological Effectiveness and Imposed Social Position," *Personnel and Guidance Journal,* Vol. 40 (1962), 418-25.

Lloyd-Jones, Esther, and Margaret R. Smith, *Student Personnel Work as Deeper Teaching.* New York: Harper & Row, Publishers, 1954.

Luijpen, William A., *Existential Phenomenology.* Pittsburgh: Duquesne University Press, 1960.

McDaniel, Henry B., and G. A. Shaftel, *Guidance in the Modern School.* New York: Dryden Press, 1956.

Maehr, Martin, and Robert Stake, "The Value Patterns of Men Who Voluntarily Quit Seminary Training," *Personnel and Guidance Journal,* Vol. 6, 537-40.

Marzolf, Stanley S., *Psychological Diagnosis and Counseling in the Schools.* New York: Holt, Rinehart & Winston, Inc., 1956.

Mathewson, Robert H., *Guidance Policy and Practice.* New York: Harper & Row, Publishers, 1955.

———, "School Guidance: A Four-Dimensional Model," *Personnel and Guidance Journal,* Vol. 8 (Apr.), 645-49.

May, Rollo, *Existence.* New York: Basic Books, Inc., 1958.

———, *Man's Search for Himself.* New York: W. W. Norton and Co., Inc., 1953.

Meadow, Lloyd, "Toward a Theory of Vocational Choice," *Journal of Counseling Psychology,* Vol. 2 (Summer 1955), 108-12.

Meehl, Paul, *Clinical Versus Statistical Prediction.* Minneapolis: University of Minnesota Press, 1954.

Miller, Frank, *Guidance Principles and Services.* Columbus, Ohio: Charles E. Merrill Books, Inc., 1961.

Miller, James G., "Toward a General Theory for the Behavioral Sciences," *American Psychologist,* Vol. 10 (Sept. 1955), 513-31.

Milliken, R. L., "Realistic Occupational Appraisal by High School Seniors," *Personnel and Guidance Journal,* Vol. 6 (Feb. 1962), 541-44.

Morse, Horace T., "General Education and Individual Guidance," *Counseling and Guidance in General Education,* ed. Melvene Hardee. Yonkers, N.Y.: World Book Company, 1955.

Mowrer, O. Hobart, "Some Constructive Features of the Concept of Sin," In Symposium: "The Role of the Concept of Sin in Psychotherapy," *Journal of Counseling Psychology,* Vol. 7 (1960), 185-88.

———, "Some Philosophical Problems in Psychological Counseling," *Journal of Counseling,* Vol. 4 (Summer 1957), 103-11.

Moynihan, James F., "The Philosophical Aspects of Guidance," *Review of Educational Research,* Vol. 27 (Apr. 1957), 186-91.

Mueller, Kate H., *Student Personnel Work in Higher Education.* Boston: Houghton Mifflin Company, 1961.

———, "Theory for Campus Discipline," *Personnel and Guidance Journal,* Vol. 36 (Jan. 1958), 302-309.

Murphy, Gardner, "The Cultural Context of Guidance," *Personnel and Guidance Journal,* Vol. 34 (Sept. 1955), 3-9.

———, and S. Guze, "Setting Limits: The Management of the Manipulative Patient," *American Journal of Psychotherapy,* Vol. 14 (1960), 30-47.

National Education Association Education Policies Commission, *Manpower and Education*. Washington, D.C.: The Commission, 1956.

Nordberg, Robert B., "Counseling: Non-Directive or Non-Coercive?" *Catholic Educational Review*, Vol. 56 (Jan. 1958), 40-44.

Nosal, Walter S., "Letters to the Editor," *Journal of Counseling Psychology*, Vol. 3 (Winter 1956), 299-302.

Nugent, Frank A., "Interest-Aptitude Congruency: A Theoretical Synthesis and a Suggested Method of Investigation," *Personnel and Guidance Journal*, Vol. 6 (Feb. 1962), 523-30.

Owen, Garnet, "Does Counseling Mean Coddling?" *Educational Forum*, Vol. 22 (Mar. 1958), 359-62.

Parody, Ovid, "An Expanding Concept of Guidance," *Teachers College Record*, Vol. 57 (May 1956), 537-45.

Paterson, Donald, "The Genesis of Modern Guidance," Reported in Farwell and Peters, *Guidance Readings for Counselors*, pp. 103-105. Chicago: Rand McNally & Company, 1960.

Patterson, C. H., *Counseling and Psychotherapy: Theory and Practice*. New York: Harper & Row, Publishers, 1959.

———, "The Counselor's Responsibility in Rehabilitation," *Journal of Rehabilitation*, Vol. 24 (Jan.-Feb. 1958), 7-11.

———, "The Place of Values in Counseling and Psychotherapy," *Journal of Counseling Psychology*, Vol. 5 (Fall 1958), 216-23.

Pepinsky, Harold B., "Productivity in the University," *Personnel and Guidance Journal*, Vol. 35 (Nov. 1956), 134-39.

———, "Research Notes for Here and There," *Journal of Counseling Psychology*, Vol. 3 (1956), 222-28.

———, and Pauline Pepinsky, *Counseling: Theory and Practice*. New York: The Ronald Press Company, 1954.

Peters, Herman, and Gail Farmwell, *Guidance: A Developmental Approach*. Chicago: Rand McNally & Company, 1959.

Rank, Otto, *Will Therapy*. New York: Alfred A. Knopf, Inc., 1936.

Renzaglia, G. A., *et al.*, "Estimation and Measurement of Personality Characteristics and Correlates of Their Congruence," *Journal of Counseling Psychology* (Spring 1962), 71-77.

Reuther, Walter, "The Crisis Before Us," *Personnel and Guidance Journal*, Vol. 36 (Sept. 1957), 4-9.

Rezler, Agnes G., "Personal Values and Achievement in College," *Personnel and Guidance Journal*, Vol. 2 (Oct. 1960), 137-43.

Robinson, Donald, and Dirck Brown, "A Report on Student Personnel Research Activities," *Personnel and Guidance Journal*, Vol. 4 (Dec. 1961), 358-60.

Roby, Thornton, "Utility and Futurity," *Behavioral Science* (Apr. 1962).

Rockwell, P. J., Jr., and J. Rothney, "Some Social Ideas of Pioneers in the Guidance Movement," *Personnel and Guidance Journal* (Dec. 1960), 349-54.

Roe, Anne, *The Psychology of Occupations*. New York: John Wiley & Sons, Inc., 1956.

Roeber, Edward C., "The President's Message," *Personnel and Guidance Journal*, Vol. 9 (May 1961), 766-67.

Rogers, Carl R., "The Characteristics of a Helping Relationship," *Personnel and Guidance Journal*, Vol. 37 (Sept. 1958), 6-16.

————, *Client-Centered Therapy*. Boston: Houghton Mifflin Company, 1951.

————, *Counseling and Psychotherapy*. Boston: Houghton Mifflin Company, 1951.

————, "A Note on 'The Nature of Man,'" *Journal of Counseling Psychology*, Vol. 4 (Fall 1957), 199-203.

————, *On Becoming a Person*. Boston: Houghton Mifflin Company, 1961.

————, "The Place of the Person in the New World of the Behavioral Sciences," *Personnel and Guidance Journal*, Vol. 6 (Feb. 1961), 442-51.

————, "Some Directions and End Points in Therapy," in *Psychotherapy: Theory and Research*, ed. O. H. Mowrer. New York: The Ronald Press Company, 1953.

————, "The Way to Do Is to Be," *Contemporary Psychology* (Spring 1959), 196-98.

————, and Rosalind Dymond, eds., *Psychotherapy and Personality Change*. Chicago: University of Chicago Press, 1954.

Rozenzweig, Saul, "Some Implicit Common Factors in Diverse Methods of Psychotherapy," *American Journal of Orthopsychiatry*, Vol. 6 (July 1936), 412-15.

Rusalem, Herbert, "New Insights on the Role of Occupational Information in Counseling," *Journal of Counseling Psychology*, Vol. 1 (Summer 1954), 84-88.

Samler, Joseph, "An Examination of Client Strength and Counselor Responsibility," *Journal of Counseling Psychology*, Vol. 1 (Spring 1962), 5-11.

————, and others, "Basic Approaches to Mental Health," *Personnel and Guidance Journal*, Vol. 37 (Sept.) 26-31; (Oct.) 114-22; (Nov.) 198-206; (Dec. 1958) 276-81; (Jan.) 342-49; (Feb.) 424-34; (Apr.) 558-68; (May 1959), 638-43.

Sanford, Nevitt, "Personality Development During the College Years," *Personnel and Guidance Journal*, Vol. 35 (Oct. 1956), 74-80.

Selden, Edward H., *"A Study of Self Structure and Level of Aspiration in Delinquent and Non-Delinquent Boys*. Unpublished doctoral dissertation. Minneapolis: University of Minnesota, 1960.

Shoben, Edward J., Jr., "Comments," (on Weitz's "Guidance as Behavioral Change," same issue), *Personnel and Guidance Journal*, Vol. 7 (Mar. 1961), 560-62.

————, "New Frontiers in Theory," *Personnel and Guidance Journal*, Vol. 32 (Oct. 1953), 80-83.

————, "Personal Responsibility, Determinism, and the Burden of Understanding," *Personnel and Guidance Journal*, Vol. 39 (1961), 342-48.

————, "A Rationale for Modern Student Personnel Work," *Personnel-o-gram*, Vol. 12, No. 3 (Mar. 1958), 10, American College Personnel Association.

————, *et al.*, "Behavior Theories and a Counseling Case: A Symposium," *Journal of Counseling Psychology*, Vol. 3 (Summer 1956), 107-24.

Shostrom, Everett L., and Lawrence M. Brammer, *The Dynamics of the Counseling Process*. New York: McGraw-Hill Book Company, Inc., 1952.

Skinner, B. F., *Walden II*. New York: The Macmillan Company, 1948.

Small, Leonard, *Personality Determinants of Vocational Choice*, Psychological Monographs, No. 351. Washington, D.C.: American Psychological Association, 1953.

Smith, M. B., "Mental Health Reconsidered: A Special Case of the Problem of Values in Psychology," *The American Psychologist*, Vol. 16 (1961), 299-306.

Snygg, Donald, and Arthur Combs, *Individual Behavior*. New York: Harper & Row, Publishers, 1949.

————, *Individual Behavior*, rev. ed. New York: Harper & Row, Publishers, 1960.

Spates, Thomas, *Human Values Where People Work*. New York: Harper & Row, Publishers, 1955.

Strang, Ruth, "Various Conceptions of Guidance," *Yearbook of Education 1955: Guidance and Counseling*, eds. R. Hall and J. Lauwerys, Sec. 6, Chap. 1, 603-37. Yonkers, N.Y.: World Book Company, 1955.

Stroup, Herbert H., "Theoretical Constructs in Student Personnel Work," *Journal of Higher Education*, Vol. 28 (June 1957), 319-26.

Super, Donald, "Career Patterns as a Basis for Vocational Counseling," *Journal of Counseling Psychology*, Vol. 1 (Feb. 1954), 12-20.

————, "A Theory of Vocational Development," *American Psychologist*, Vol. 8 (May 1953), 185-90.

————, "Transition: From Vocational Guidance to Counseling Psychology," *Journal of Counseling Psychology*, Vol. 2 (Spring 1955), 3-9.

Thompson, Albert S., "A Rationale for Vocational Guidance," *Personnel and Guidance Journal*, Vol. 32 (May 1954), 533-35.

Tiedeman, David V., and Joseph G. Bryan, "Prediction of College Field of Concentration," *Harvard Educational Review*, Vol. 24 (Spring 1954), 122-39.

Tompkins, W. L., "Blamed If You Do, and Blamed If You Don't!" *Journal of the National Association of Women Deans and Counselors*, Vol. 21 (Jan. 1958), 74-77.

Tyler, Leona, "Minimum Change Therapy," *Personnel and Guidance Journal*, Vol. 38 (1960), 475-79.

———, "Theoretical Principles Underlying the Counseling Process," *Journal of Counseling Psychology*, Vol. 5 (Spring 1958), 3-8.

Walker, Donald E., "Carl Rogers and the Nature of Man," *Journal of Counseling Psychology*, Vol. 3 (Summer 1956), 89-92.

Walters, Orville S., "Metaphysics, Religion, and Psychotherapy," *Journal of Counseling Psychology*, Vol. 5 (Winter 1958), 243-52.

Weitz, Henry, "Counseling as a Function of the Counselor's Personality," *Personnel and Guidance Journal*, Vol. 35 (Jan. 1957), 276-80.

———, "Guidance as Behavior Change," *Personnel and Guidance Journal*, Vol. 7 (Mar. 1961), 550-60.

Wilkins, William D., and Barbara J. Perlmutter, "The Philosophical Foundations of Guidance and Personnel Work," *Review of Educational Research*, XXX, 2 (Apr. 1960), 97-104.

Williamson, Edmund G., *Student Personnel Services in Colleges and Universities*. New York: McGraw-Hill Book Company, Inc., 1961.

———, "Student Personnel Work," *Encyclopedia of Educational Research*, ed. Walter S. Monroe, rev. ed., pp. 1290-92. New York: Macmillan Company, 1950.

———, "Value Orientation in Counseling," *Personnel and Guidance Journal*, Vol. 36 (Apr. 1958), 520-28.

———, and J. G. Darley, *Introduction to Student Personnel Work*. New York: McGraw-Hill Book Company, Inc., 1937.

Wise, W. M., "Student Personnel Work—Future Trends," *Personnel and Guidance Journal*, Vol. 9 (May 1961), 704-709.

Wolfle, Dael L., "Guidance and Educational Strategy," *Personnel and Guidance Journal*, Vol. 37 (Sept. 1958), 17-25.

Wrenn, C. Gilbert, "Philosophical and Psychological Bases of Personnel Services in Education," *Personnel Services in Education*. Fifty-eighth Yearbook of the National Society for the Study of Education, Part II, Chap. 3, pp. 41-81. Chicago: University of Chicago Press, 1959.

———, "The Self Concept in Counseling," *Journal of Counseling Psychology*, Vol. 5 (Summer 1958), 104-109.

———, "Some Emotional Factors in Counseling," Chap. VI, *Guidance in the Age of Automation*. Syracuse: Syracuse University Press, 1957.

———, "Status and Role of the School Counselor," *Personnel and Guidance Journal*, Vol. 36 (Nov. 1957), 175-83.

———, *Student Personnel Work in College*. New York: The Ronald Press Company, 1951.

Selected Bibliography

PART II

Barnes, Hazel E., *The Literature of Possibility*. Lincoln: University of Nebraska Press, 1959.

Barrett, William, *Irrational Man*. Garden City, N.Y.: Doubleday & Company, Inc., 1958.

Binswanger, Ludwig, "Existential Analysis and Psychotherapy," in Fromm-Reichman and J. Moreno, eds., *Progress in Psychotherapy*, pp. 144-48. New York: Grune & Stratton, Inc., 1956.

——, "On the Relationship Between Husserl's Phenomenology and Psychological Insight," *Philosophical and Phenomenological Research* (1941), pp. 199-210.

Boss, M., *Meaning and Content of Sexual Perversions: A Daseinanalytic Approach to the Psychopathology of the Phenomenon of Love*. New York: Grune & Stratton, Inc., 1949.

Buber, Martin, *Between Man and Man*. Boston: Beacon Press, 1955.

——, *I and Thou*. New York: Charles Scribner's Sons, 1958.

Buytendijk, F. J. J, "Experienced Freedom and Moral Freedom in the Child's Consciousness," *Educational Theory* (1953), pp. 1-13.

——, "The Function of the Parts Within the Structure of the Whole," *Journal of Individual Psychology* (1959), pp. 15, 73-78.

Cochrane, Arthur, *The Existentialists and God*. Philadelphia: The Westminster Press, 1956.

Creegan, Robert F., "Phenomenology," in P. J. Harriman, ed., *Encyclopedia of Psychology*, pp. 512-15. New York: Citadel Press, 1946.

Edel, May, and Abraham Edel, *Anthropology and Ethics*. Springfield, Ill.: Charles C Thomas, 1959.

Feigl, Herbert, and May Brodbeck, eds., *Readings in the Philosophy of Science*. New York: Appleton-Century-Crofts, 1953.

Feuer, Lewis S., *Psychoanalysis and Ethics*. Springfield, Ill.: Charles C Thomas, 1955.

Frankl, Viktor, *The Doctor and the Soul: An Introduction to Logotherapy*. New York: Alfred A. Knopf, Inc., 1955.

——, *From Death Camp to Existentialism*. Boston: Beacon Press, 1959.

Freeman, Kenneth J., *Schools of Hellas*. London: Macmillan and Company, Ltd., 1922.

Fromm, Erich, *Man for Himself*. New York: Holt, Rinehart & Winston, Inc., 1947.

Gibson, Walker, ed., *The Limits of Language*. New York: Hill and Wang, Inc., 1962.

Harriman, Philip L., *Encyclopedia of Psychology*. New York: Citadel Press, 1946.

Heidegger, Martin, *Existence and Being*. Chicago: Henry Regnery Company, 1949. (English Translation of Heidegger's *Sein und Zeit*.)

Husserl, Edmund, "Phenomenology," *Encyclopaedia Britannica*, 14th ed.

Kaufmann, W. A., ed., *Existentialism from Dostoevsky to Sartre*. New York: Meridian Books, Inc., 1956.

Kuenzli, Alfred, ed., *The Phenomenological Problem*. New York: Harper & Row, Publishers, 1959.

Lamont, W. D., *The Value Judgment*. Edinburgh: The University Press, 1955.

Luipjen, William A., *Existential Phenomenology*. Pittsburgh: Duquesne University Press, 1960.

Malinowski, Bronislaw, *Magic, Science, and Religion*. Boston: The Beacon Press, 1948.

Marcel, Gabriel, *The Philosophy of Existence*. London: Harvill, 1948.

May, Rollo, *Man's Search for Himself*. New York: W. W. Norton, 1953.

————, *et al.*, *Existence: A New Dimension in Psychiatry and Psychology*. New York: Basic Books, Inc., 1958.

————, *Existential Psychology*. New York: Random House, 1961.

Morris, Van Cleve, "Existentialism and the Education of Twentieth Century Man," *Educational Theory* (Jan. 1961), pp. 52-60.

Nettelship, R. L., *The Theory of Education in Plato's Republic*. Oxford: The Clarendon Press, 1935.

Nowell-Smith, P. H., *Ethics*. London: George Allen & Unwin, 1954.

Opler, Marvin, *Culture, Psychiatry, and Human Values*. Springfield, Ill.: Charles C Thomas, 1956.

Reik, Theodor, *Listening with the Third Ear*. New York: Farrar, Straus, 1948.

Sartre, Jean-Paul, *Existentialism*. New York: Philosophical Library, 1947.

Smith, B. O., and R. Ennis, *Language and Concepts in Education*. Chicago: Rand McNally Company, 1961.

Stevenson, Charles L., *Ethics and Language*. New Haven: Yale University Press, 1944.

Titus, Harold, *Ethics for Today*. New York: American Book Company, 1957.

————, *Living Issues in Philosophy*. New York: American Book Company, 1959.

Urban, W. B., *Beyond Realism and Idealism*. London: George Allen & Unwin, 1949.

Van den Berg, J. H., *The Phenomenological Approach to Psychiatry*.
    Springfield, Ill.: Charles C Thomas, 1955.
Wahl, Jean, *A Short History of Existentialism*. New York: Philosophical
    Library, 1949.

Indexes

Biographical Index

A

Alcuin, 16

Allport, Gordon, 5, 30, 45, 46, 99, 121, 122

Arbuckle, Dugald S., 31, 38, 45, 47, 48

Aristotle, 14

B

Bally, G., 107

Barry, Ruth, 23

Benezet, Louis T., 31

Berdyaev, Nicolai, 105, 110, 117

Berger, Emanuel, 48

Binswanger, Ludwig, 37, 107

Bordin, Edward S., 34, 39, 93

Borow, Henry, 97-100

Boss, M., 107

Brady, Dominic, 144

Brown, Dirck, 43

Buber, Martin, 117, 119

Buytendijk, F. J., 107

C

Charlemagne, 15-17

Cheever, Ezekiel, 19

Combs, Arthur W., 35, 36, 66, 67, 70, 71, 75, 76, 81, 82, 87, 109, 111, 140, 144

Cotton, John, 19

Cribbin, James, 3-5, 30, 31, 33, 78, 79, 80, 81, 131, 144

Curran, Charles, 31, 46, 47

D

Dewey, John, 6, 21, 30, 32, 36, 37, 59, 75, 76

Dilworth, Thomas, 19

Dostoievsky, Fyodor, 112

Dressel, Paul, 32, 38

Dreyfus, Edward, 48, 106

Dugan, Willis E., 38

Dupuis, Adrian, 45, 47

E

Edwards, Jonathan, 19-21

F

Feigl, Herbert, 70

Fisher, Margaret, 47

Ford, E., 47

Franklin, Benjamin, 21, 124

Freud, Sigmund, 25, 57, 140

Froehlich, Clifford P., 47

Fromm, Eric, 80

G

Gillespie, R., 9

Ginsberg, Eli, 43

Glanz, Edward, 45

Gleason, Robert, 38

Gruen, Walter, 46

Guze, S., 47

H

Hagmaier, George, 38

Hall, G. Stanley, 25

Hardee, Melvene, 31, 32

Harris, W. T., 21

Harrison, Edna L., 41, 99

Heidegger, Martin, 105, 107, 110

Henderson, D., 9

Hitchcock, A. A., 23

Hobbs, N., 40

Holt, Edwin, 140

Hull, 122

Husserl, E., 122

J

Jacob, P., 80

James, William, 21, 129

163

General Index

A

Abilities, variance in, 13
Advancement, in Plato's school, 12
Advice, 11, 115
Aesthetic stage, 119
Afterlife, 21
Agreements, Cribbin's listing of, 30
Aid, mutual, 21, 135
Aims, proximate, 79, 80
Aims, ultimate, 79, 80
Amorphous stage, 55, 56
Anguish, 112
Anthropomorphism, 10
Anxiety, 21, 30, 131, 135
    choice, 113, 135
    existential, 48, 106, 121
    pathological, 48
Apprenticeship, 17
Archetype, 13
Aristocracy, 15
Army Alpha test, 26
Army Beta test, 26
Articles, philosophical (1952-1957), 30
Articles, philosophical (1958-1960), 38
Assumptions, common to textbooks,
    78
    of guidance identified, 30, 41, 42
    of Leibniz, 122, 123
    of Locke, 122
    of non-directive counseling, 64, 65,
    56
    of phenomenology, 71, 72
    of Plato, 13
Athenians, opposition to Plato, 14
Authority, "given," 15

B

Beauty, 12
Behavior, factors in, 48
Behavior, human model, 80
Behaviorism, 46, 81, 106, 121
Beliefs, held by student personnel
    workers, 54

Beta test, Army, 26
British Poor Laws, 17
Buddhism, 48

C

Caste, under Charlemagne, 15
Catharsis, 57, 82
Cause and effect, 62, 82, 104, 133, 134,
    140, 145
Change, 75, 83, 140, 143, 145, 146
Character training, 22
Choice:
    freedom of, 21, 30, 120, 123, 125,
    127, 142, 144, 145, 146
    a sham, 41, 46, 66, 67, 81, 84, 112
Choice-making, 57, 87, 103, 110, 112,
    114, 125, 126, 133, 134, 135, 136,
    145, 146
Christianity, 117
    enemies of, 118
    in education, 19
Christians, early, 15, 16
Class, under Charlemagne, 15, 16
Client-centered therapy, 30
Clinical counseling, 32, 59
Colonial education, 19
Commitment, of counselor, 41, 59
    need for, 110-112, 114, 121, 133, 135
Condition, human, 97, 114, 132
Conditioning, 42
Confidentiality, 43
Confirmability of hypotheses, 69
Conformity, 80
Conscious mind, 58
Contemplation, 13
Contribution to philosophical litera-
    ture, 35, 38
Correspondence theory of truth, 24,
    41, 85, 140, 141, 146
Counseling,
    based on Sartre's ideas, 116, 117
    educational, 12
    existential, 124, 125

166